THE
MASTERPIECE PRICE
BOOK 6 REFLECTIONS OF GOD MOMENTS

DEDICATION

To all of those who have been broken and remade into His image through trials and hardships, this book is dedicated to you. I have watched the journey of so many and felt the hands of kinship and love in you as we journey together through the tough and rough places. Kelley, thank you for being the editor and motivator in these last months. Angel, you are an inspiration-keep fighting! Gina, keep going on through this too! Ashley, your art speaks healing to the broken. Angela, your constancy is bracing. Joan, your steadfastness is inspiring. Teresa, your peace in all is a gift.
Kaylen, you are a gift-a princess of high price and value to me.

I dedicate this book to each of you mentioned and not mentioned who inspire and keep fighting the fight, to become the Masterpiece He has paid the price for through your trials. He has paid it all so you can be an overcomer.

The Masterpiece Price
Book 6 Reflections of God Moments
56 One Minute Devotionals
copyright © 2024

Written by: Donesa Walker
Design by: Will Baten

CONTENTS

I love you, God—
you make me strong.
God is bedrock under my feet,
the castle in which I live,
my rescuing knight.
My God—the high crag
where I run for dear life,
hiding behind the boulders,
safe in the granite hideout.

A hostile world! I call to God,
I cry to God to help me.
From his palace he hears my call;
my cry brings me right into his presence—
a private audience!

But me he caught—reached all the way
from sky to sea; he pulled me out
Of that ocean of hate, that enemy chaos,
the void in which I was drowning.
They hit me when I was down,
but God stuck by me.
He stood me up on a wide-open field;
I stood there saved—surprised to be loved!

What a God! His road
stretches straight and smooth.
Every God-direction is road-tested.
Everyone who runs toward him
Makes it.

Psalms 18: 1-3, 6, 16-19, 30

4

THE MOUNTAIN OF PRAISE!

David wrote this Psalm in the midst of a battle for his life. Saul was pursuing him, angry at him for becoming more loved by the people and anointed by God. David didn't have an in person visit from God in the flesh. He wasn't more loved by God than you are but God called him a man after God's heart because he ran after God's heart. He chased God's presence in the good times and the bad. The psalms are a collection of his songs throughout his life. Yesterday, my pastor made a point that struck me. We spend the majority of our lives on the side of the mountain feeding on God's word, seeking His presence, running to Him to hide in the high crags towards the top of the mountain. The valley is the place we go to draw others to him for that's where many are and then we travel together to the mountaintop. The rains and storms of life come while we are traveling in this life. A rainbow is God's promise never to flood the earth again but it is also a promise of His presence.

You see a rainbow can only be formed when light is refracted. The white light of His Sonlight refracted through the storms of our lives is what brings the promise of His presence. The key to this is what David embraced. This is why he ran after God's heart. David knew that God's presence comes from our praise, our cry, our reaching out to Him. God on the mountain is still God in the valley. Although you may feel like you are drowning in an ocean of waves pounding you, you have the ability to refract His Sonlight calling upon His promises just by opening your mouth and beginning to praise. Feel too down, click on worship songs and let them begin to fill you. Stuck on the side of the mountain hiding behind the rocks of safety in His arms? Feeling bereft and empty? Hurting beyond your imagination? Discouraged by all that's happening around you? These are storms and yes they are dark. The hailstorms are throwing their worst in the hurricane of life...but there is still Sonlight waiting to be refracted into His promises. No matter how dark the cave, how deep the ocean or how dire your circumstances, His Sonlight is there waiting on you. Begin refracting it with praise. Watch what happens as you chase His heart...His promises begin to spill into you and before you know it, you have made the journey to the top of the mountain. Refresh there a little while then get going for another storm is approaching and there is someone in the valley who is needing you to be that piece of Sonlight refracted into their darkness so they can grab hold and begin to refract it themselves.

Since this is the kind of life we have chosen, the life of the Spirit, let us make sure that we do not just hold it as an idea in our heads or a sentiment in our hearts, but work out its implications in every detail of our lives. That means we will not compare ourselves with each other as if one of us were better and another worse. We have far more interesting things to do with our lives. Each of us is an original.

Galatians 5: 25-26

UNIQUE AND ADORED!

In this verse, God confirms that each of us is unique but still made in His image. In a sea of tulips, they may all look the same but each one is unique and unfolds in its own time. Our lives like a flower are each unique and God unfolds the events in His timing. We often forget how much He loves us especially when anger or hurt builds up for something He didn't do on our time table like the loss of a loved one. But this is our assurance that He who is doing a good work in us is able to complete it. Jesus is coming soon to catch his bride away. Are you ready?

Because of the extravagance of those revelations, and so I wouldn't get a big head, I was given the gift of a handicap to keep me in constant touch with my limitations. Satan's angel did his best to get me down; what he in fact did was push me to my knees. No danger then of walking around high and mighty! At first I didn't think of it as a gift, and begged God to remove it. Three times I did that, and then he told me,

My grace is enough; it's all you need.

My strength comes into its own in your weakness.

Once I heard that, I was glad to let it happen. I quit focusing on the handicap and began appreciating the gift. It was a case of Christ's strength moving in on my weakness. Now I take limitations in stride, and with good cheer, these limitations that cut me down to size—abuse, accidents, opposition, bad breaks. I just let Christ take over! And so the weaker I get, the stronger I become.

2 Corinthians 12: 7-10

EMBRACING LIMITATIONS!

Honestly, this is the second time I have typed these words because my clumsy hand deleted the first after I had typed them all before. As I sit here, I am in pain in my back and my hands are numb, my ears are ringing and I don't feel like worshiping but I know in my heart that it is through praise that I get victory! Paul was writing these words to the church at Corinth telling his story and as I asked for God's healing to come over me today...He said these words to me...my grace is enough. I said yes Lord I understand but I am believing for a miracle of healing...then I opened up His word and this is where He led me. Paul's story of learning to embrace the place you are at as His strength being enough. Don't get me wrong, I believe in miracles! I completely have seen these in my own life so much. I've seen blind eyes opened, some through the miracle of medicine and surgery and some through instant miraculous healing. I've seen cancers healed both ways in my own life and my parents' lives. I've seen and experienced dry bones living again (I have a cadaver bone in my spine which is now alive again working with my body to build my new spine). I've seen miracles of healing through intense exercises of faith and intensely exercising the brain at my office. But there is a truth that God is saying through Paul here that we must embrace. In this world, this imperfect earthly planet, we will have troubles, pains, death, sickness but we are not of this world. I must admit that I have worked very hard in life with the medical professionals to remain here...I've had over 19 surgeries and countless other procedures but I am so blessed as God has seen fit to continue to use me here. God has given me the extravagance of His grace. He has seen fit to give me limitations like weights on a hot air balloon so that I can embrace His strength in my weakness and understand that His grace is made perfect in my limits.

The power of God is perfected in our weaknesses because then and only then can we understand our own limitations and present ourselves in His strength so we may walk fully in Him. We fight so hard to embrace the reality of these fading bodies that we often fail to grasp the reality of His presence. We are not made for this world. We are a vapor in the wind yet He chooses us to walk through and in our weaknesses so His strength is made perfect. Stop. Think. We all have struggles in this life. There is no one perfect. The social media perfection doesn't exist. His mightiness isn't in our strength but instead when we embrace our limitations in favor of His strength.

Lord, I am embracing my limitations today as a source of your strength. I will walk in your grace and not my own abilities.

The revelation of God is whole
and pulls our lives together.
The signposts of God are clear
and point out the right road.
The life-maps of God are right,
showing the way to joy.
The directions of God are plain
and easy on the eyes.
God's reputation is twenty-four-carat gold,
with a lifetime guarantee.
The decisions of God are accurate
down to the nth degree.
God's Word is better than a diamond,
better than a diamond set between emeralds.
You'll like it better than strawberries in spring,
better than red, ripe strawberries.

Psalms 19: 7-10

JESUS AT THE CENTER!

Jesus at the Center of it ALL!

Just a few months ago, Wes drove me to Colorado on a business trip and we decided to go a different direction than usual. Wes studied the maps and made a plan. We loaded up, headed out and turned on the GPS system. A few hours later, in frustration, Wes remarked that he was irritated that we were on the wrong road because he had listened to the tech instead of what he knew from studying the maps. This morning as I read, God spoke this to my heart about being misled by the new fangled traps of the world when I know the revelation of God for truth. I know the way to joy because He directs me from within to choose it. I don't have to wander in frustration because I can clearly read the signs all around me declaring His handiwork. I have His revelation easily accessible (The Bible) in my hand and His revelation is perfect and true.

I've watched these different programs where people are digging for gold or diamonds and they spend their whole lives and all their money seeking it...God's word is better than gold and diamonds. By far, it is a more secure investment as God is the financial advisor there and knows our every need before we think or ask. God decisions are 100% accurate all the way through to eternity. Because they are the path to eternity. Oftentimes, we get caught up in our own thinking and we begin to rely on the opinions of others rather than the convictions of what we know He has placed within us as we studied His word. We allow fear of the unknown place to direct us into using resources or paths not of Him. But just like Wes & I on that trip, all befuddled and lost...Wes said look for the signs. Turn off that noise and look for the signs. The map is clear. We studied the path and knew the roads to travel...we just needed to follow the signposts clearly posted and quickly we got back on track. God's reputation is one you can trust. His paths are clearly marked with signposts. We must press in and trust. We must turn off the noise around us trying to redirect us in circles and follow the signposts of His love & direction.
The sweetest flavor like that of a strawberry ripe from the field awaits our arrival...taste and see...God is good. Put Jesus at the center of it all and let Him direct you. He said that He is the way, the truth and the life and no man can come to the Father except through Him. Turn off the noise, tune into the God Positioning System...read His word, look for His signs, follow His path...then your way will be straight and clear.

THE VIEWFINDER!

Each picture zooms in a little closer...what for some is a weed or nuisance, for others is a thing of beauty, or a source of sustenance or even a future for the person who sees it as a nuisance or weed in their lives. Bees bring about pollination that ultimately allows food to grow! This bush which if not controlled can become a huge problem even a parasitic death to the trees around it; when controlled, it becomes a source of food in my future. What you cannot see is that just beyond this bush in my yard, is a garden of vegetables awaiting the pollination that these bees will supply. Bringing sustainability to my vegetables means sometimes I have to control the weeds so they don't take over but allow their beauty to supply a fragrance and source while carefully maintained. Some people are like this in our lives. They are a source of irritation to some that will ultimately bring about fruit in that person's life but you gotta control the growth. Too much can become parasitic, too little can threaten your own potential. Don't let the things that irritate you become a parasitic bitterness. Rather find the beauty and fragrance in them, allow them to pollinate your garden and allow the Master Gardener to guide you to control their overgrowth!

"Don't pick on people, jump on their failures, criticize their faults—unless, of course, you want the same treatment. Don't condemn those who are down; that hardness can boomerang. Be easy on people; you'll find life a lot easier. Give away your life; you'll find life given back, but not merely given back—given back with bonus and blessing. Giving, not getting, is the way. Generosity begets generosity."

Luke 6: 37-38

THE CIRCUMSTANCES OF JOY!

Because He lives I can face tomorrow...because I know His promises...Life doesn't always dish out fairly. I used to tell my students...Life isn't fair...get over it and move on to your purpose...treating others poorly when they are down is no different than kicking a puppy. Hardness towards people in their unique situations will come back on you. Luke was a physician and he saw people who were hurting. He also had a gentle nature and was pretty easy going from what history records. I imagine dealing with all those big personalities surrounding Jesus was an interesting thing to do. Living a life of criticizing and finding fault is honestly exhausting. Mentally, looking for the good in each moment gives a life of peace and fulfillment because it drives you to seek God's presence in each thing.

Wes tells me of things I did and said when I was in the hospital that are so out of character for me that I find them embarrassing but he also said that no matter what, I was never ugly which brings me relief. When a person loses themselves due to illness or medication or situations, they sometimes forget their way. They may do, act, say things that are out of character. When these things happen, it isn't the time to lose patience for that may be a teaching moment for you. When someone is down, find a way to serve them because by doing so you will be blessed yourself.

Think of all the joys & gifts you have. Find delight in your day. If you feel frustrated with another, look at them and find something positive and uplifting about them that you can hang your hat on. Don't allow the spirit of defeat or anger to push you into treating them badly. Disappointment often times causes us to lash out in frustration. I am so guilty of this. Instead, let's refocus on Because He Lives...your disappointment with your circumstances pales beside His sacrifice and His resurrection. When you want to say something negative, start to sing Because He Lives...I guarantee it will change your perspective. I am a glass half full person but I am surrounded oftentimes by glass half empty...or with not enough water to do anything with people. This is mostly because situations and circumstances have gotten to them. They have allowed the circumstances to steal their joy. I had this happen to me before and I determined it would not happen again because my joy that I have wasn't given to me by my circumstances so I'm not giving up my joy to my situations. This joy that I have is all because of Jesus...because He lives. So begin to sing...let joy rise...no matter who or what is pressing in on you. Give...when you have nothing else to give...begin to generously pour of yourself into others allowing God's river to flow through you into others washing you clean of the criticizing and angry spirit...allow Him to move you into who He is...Because

He Lives and He's coming soon!

So, friends, we can now—without hesitation—walk right up to God, into "the Holy Place." Jesus has cleared the way by the blood of his sacrifice, acting as our priest before God. The "curtain" into God's presence is his body. So let's do it—full of belief, confident that we're presentable inside and out.
Let's keep a firm grip on the promises that keep us going. He always keeps his word. Let's see how inventive we can be in encouraging love and helping out, not avoiding worshiping together as some do but spurring each other on, especially as we see the big Day approaching.

Hebrews 10: 19-25

BEING KNOWN AS I AM!

Backstage passes, celebrity status and cheerleading...all have one thing in common...intimacy. Connection. A few years ago, I was at an event and I saw a crowd gathering and whispering in excited voices about "her". They were so filled with admiration and awe that I had to see what or who they were excited to see. Imagine my surprise when I walked over to see who they were talking about and it was my sister. Her star power had put all of them in the throes of passionate excitement but to me, she was my sister...I was blessed with an intimacy that I didn't even realize was valuable. I had her cell, I could text or call her any time. Honestly, I did not value that access until I saw that value through another's eyes. The disciples had the same problem. They had intimacy with the King of Glory but they underestimated its value. They walked, talked and dined with Him and yet never quite grasped who He was. Today, we have intimate access to The Creator of the entire Universe. We have access to the King who owns everything we see and cannot see. We know the Savior of the whole world and yet we devalue this intimacy. We fail to recognize His authority and our connection.

Paul encourages us to understand the value of this intimacy and ability to walk right into the throne room of God knowing that He will hear us, meet us, and supply our every need according to His glory. If I told you today that you could meet the Queen of England or some special celebrity, you would go out of your way to find the right clothing and tell everyone in excitement about your special audience.

But as I sit here in awe of my King, I do not find a fancy outfit to put on because He has provided me with a garment of praise. As I confidently come into His presence, I know He will be there. He won't stand me up for someone more important than I. I know His words are true and His promises are rock solid. I know He has prepared a table of awesomeness for me full of rich food of the Word. I feel His loving arms around me welcoming me into His presence. I am the celebrity of the moment and this King of all creation has welcomed me cheering me on. I am humbled and awed that He who takes such good care of me is willing to take time out of His busyness to dine with me.

How often I forget as my day rushes forward of the thrill and the values of this intimacy. You see this intimacy came at the highest price. The sacrifice of the Prince of Peace upon an altar of selfish pomposity was the ultimate price. It is a debt that I cannot pay but it has already been paid. How can I who owes so much fail to recognize the value of His forgiveness? And yet I do. The Big Reveal is about to happen. The moment is approaching when my intimacy with Him will be revealed for all to see.

There's more to come: We continue to shout our praise even when we're hemmed in with troubles, because we know how troubles can develop passionate patience in us, and how that patience in turn forges the tempered steel of virtue, keeping us alert for whatever God will do next. In alert expectancy such as this, we're never left feeling shortchanged. Quite the contrary—we can't round up enough containers to hold everything God generously pours into our lives through the Holy Spirit!

Romans 5: 3-5

Tempering is a process of heat treating, which is used to increase the toughness of iron-based alloys. Tempering is usually performed after hardening, to reduce some of the excess hardness, and is done by heating the metal to some temperature below the critical point for a certain period of time, then allowing it to cool in still air. The exact temperature determines the amount of hardness removed, and depends on both the specific composition of the alloy and on the desired properties in the finished product. For instance, very hard tools are often tempered at low temperatures, while springs are tempered at much higher temperatures.

THERE'S MORE TO COME!

That's shouting ground! God of the mountains is still God in the valleys!
Paul is writing to the church in Rome from prison saying that God is using things that require lots of patience for the purpose of forging them into the tempered steel of virtue...so they can be ready and alert for what's next...he has an attitude of expectation and alludes to the story of the woman with the oil in the Old Testament who collected containers to fill with oil because God kept the oil flowing as long as she was pouring out...

Paul is telling us that our situation doesn't determine God's ability. God uses situational things to make us stronger and more resilient for His purposes. A tempered steel blade is stronger because it is able to weather the blows without breaking as it has a little give in it to handle the hits. If the steel is hardened too much it becomes so unbending that it cannot withstand blows and cracks.
Think about that for a minute.

Passionate patience. That's the bend we develop in the storms of life. We learn that the storms are just the place before the miracle. The situation is the circumstances of life but the God of the mountain has provided the oil. We just need to start collecting the containers of expectation for His outpouring. In a state of alert expectation, you are not caught off guard nor left feeling left out or short changed but rather excited to see what He is going to do.

The flower in this picture is a flower of war. The flower is in Ukraine in a friend's garden. It is blooming in expectation in the middle of the bombings and it isn't worried. The quiet confidence of this flower blooming when no one has tended it nor watered it and it has endured the conflict. This resilience is what God wants from us. He wants us to have an energetic expectation of what He is about to do. We must still go about collecting the containers of life as we prepare for His outpouring though. Do what He has set before you in an air of expectation because He has already told the oil to keep producing. He has already set the things in motion for your miracle! You need to step out now in His promises knowing that He has good things in store as He tempers you through this experience. Lord let me have your passionate patience as I wait in expectation for your outpouring. I will not be idle but will be out gathering your containers so that you may fill us all with your oil of gladness, joy, mercy, love, and all that you would give for us to be used by you as a vessel of your using. A tempered steel sword to fight the battles ahead. God of the day...I thank you for being God of the night as well!

"Don't let this rattle you. You trust God, don't you? Trust me. There is plenty of room for you in my Father's home. If that weren't so, would I have told you that I'm on my way to get a room ready for you? And if I'm on my way to get your room ready, I'll come back and get you so you can live where I live. And you already know the road I'm taking."

"Believe me: I am in my Father and my Father is in me. If you can't believe that, believe what you see—these works. The person who trusts me will not only do what I'm doing but even greater things, because I, on my way to the Father, am giving you the same work to do that I've been doing. You can count on it. From now on, whatever you request along the lines of who I am and what I am doing, I'll do it. That's how the Father will be seen for who he is in the Son. I mean it. Whatever you request in this way, I'll do.

John 14: 1-4, 11-14

PARCHED BUT GROWING!

"April showers bring May flowers." At least that's the saying as Spring brings an inconsistent weather pattern to us. I sit here listening to the rain and knowing it is necessary to water the crops and fields and yards and bathe the animals, freshen the waters, etc. In our busy lives, rain and all of the abundance it brings along with the uncertainty has become an inconvenience. We don't think we rely on it in our everyday lives as we have running water and yet we do. We have become so adapted to our ways and our conveniences that we have forgotten what is necessary to sustain life.

Jesus is speaking to the disciples in this passage instructing them before his crucifixion. He's not telling them that God is a genie in a bottle going around granting wishes like many think but rather that God dwells in the heart, mind, and soul of the believer who places trust in Him. Jesus is telling them that the God of all power was sending another to dwell in us to give us authority and a channel directly to the God of all creation to perform the same miracles and wonders that Jesus did through the same God connection. He came as the path, the road, the way.

As the rain falls, it collects together on the ground forming streams as it runs through the course set by the highs/lows of the ground, however, the more water there is, the greater potential there is to cut new paths, channels, etc. as the trickle becomes a stream then becomes a current like a river and as more water runs together, it becomes more and more of a powerful force changing landscapes around it. God is this river of life and channel of change in us. He charges us to water the lives of the people around us with His grace and mercy. He instructs us to be the river of change by taking in more of Him and flowing together in Him so that the power of the Holy Spirit whom He sent can embolden us to do greater things.

A drop of water may seem powerless and without much potential but that same drop can save a plant or a person, collect nourishment from the resources and carry it to where it is needed. That same drop can change into a hailstone or be driven by the wind, it can become a snowflake or an ice pellet. That same drop that fell from the sky can be used over and over as it submits to the cycle of nature that God set forth.

In this passage, Jesus asks an important question: Do you trust God? He doesn't wait for the answer but rather proceeds on with His thoughts and instructions that we are to Trust Him also because they are one and those who trust in Him become one with Him... aligned in Him using the power of His authority to do mighty things through Him.

The inconvenience of the rain is really a way to call our attention to a necessity in our lives. Rain changes our normal patterns. We have to slow down, get our rain gear out and change our plans in order to stay dry. God allows and causes things to come into our lives to direct us, change us, move us into His will and His ways. We are a drop of water wielded by the Master of the Wind. We can yield to His hand and become a part of the powerful changing waters or we can just be a drop of water wielded and used up because we choose to not be directed and used by Him. You cannot change your birth but you can choose your existence to be a tool of the Master. Yielded. That's where the power is. Do you trust God? If the answer is yes, then all His authority is in your keeping and through His direction you can become the power of change in your world. Yielded to be a single drop of water bound to Him for His purposes whether that be a snowflake in a snowball or in an avalanche...whether that be a single drop in a river of change or the droplet that brings life to a parched soul. Yielded... that's the key and the answer to the question. The promise is there. Jesus is preparing a place for you and He's coming soon. Don't let your situation throw you! Trust Him. Through Him you have the power and authority to move in magnificent ways. A single drop of water in the Master's hand has power beyond imagination. Lord, I want to be used by you, A holy example of your authority. I desire to be a single droplet of Holy water directed through you into a powerful current of change. I yield my life into your direction today as I see every raindrop in a new light of your glory and power. I choose today to become what you would direct my life to be.

"This is the crisis we're in: God-light streamed into the world, but men and women everywhere ran for the darkness. They went for the darkness because they were not really interested in pleasing God. Everyone who makes a practice of doing evil, addicted to denial and illusion, hates God-light and won't come near it, fearing a painful exposure. But anyone working and living in truth and reality welcomes God-light so the work can be seen for the God-work it is."

"The One that God sent speaks God's words. And don't think he rations out the Spirit in bits and pieces. The Father loves the Son extravagantly. He turned everything over to him so he could give it away—a lavish distribution of gifts. That is why whoever accepts and trusts the Son gets in on everything, life complete and forever! And that is also why the person who avoids and distrusts the Son is in the dark and doesn't see life. All he experiences of God is darkness, and an angry darkness at that."

John 3: 19-21, 34-36

SCATTERED BY THE LIGHT!

My confession: I cannot stand bugs! I know they have value and such but yuck, especially roaches. One thing I know about bugs from a personal perspective is that when a light is on they are either drawn to it or skitter away from it. Interestingly enough, the bugs that fly usually are drawn to it while those that crawl on the ground usually avoid it. Why? Altitude and dependencies. You see those that are on the ground are used to dwelling in the dark earth and light exposes them and is painful to them as then they can be seen and killed so they fear the light.

In these first verses, Jesus is speaking about Himself. He came streaming light into the world (literally as the Star of Bethlehem shone over Him at birth). But those in the power of darkness ran like cockroaches trying to shut His light down because they feared exposure. This is why the attack on the church will become more and more obvious as God's light shines. The closer you draw to God, the more you reflect His light, the further those bound in darkness will appear as they skitter away...fearing exposure. But what about those drawn to the light, those that flutter near risking all to be near the warmth, drawn to its presence. These are the harvest. These are the ones that God is drawing to the Light.

Bright lights reveal flaws. Recently I had my son replace 5 burned out bulbs in my bathroom. Wow! The difference was astounding! You see there were 9 bulbs in there but over time only 4 continued to work and I became accustomed to that. I got used to only a little light, like only fellowshipping through online service or occasional video Sunday school classes because it reveals less of the truth and that is comfortable. But Jesus didn't come to bring a little light and if the bulbs won't do their jobs in the place He has put them to function then He will replace them with fresh ones that are passionately shining His light. The truth is that more Light reveals cracks and crannies we have hidden or allowed to become dusty and grimy stained with sin and that's not fun because it means we must do something about it. Cleaning up our old hidden messes isn't fun. It's humbling, revealing and often painful.

This is the difference: in the first part of these verses you see Jesus speaking that the Godlight/Sonlight streaming reveals and exposes sin but those who are not in sin welcome it and are drawn to it soaking Him in. Then you see John speaking as he came before Jesus to prepare the way...John lets us in on the secret...the Light of God is His extravagant love! He loves so much that it's not a single flashlight bulb looking into our lives but a Sonbeam! It's not rationed but extraordinary. This intense over the top love came to earth as a baby and died on a cross for our sins then rose again so we might have eternal Light & Life. Life isn't good without light and light is no good without life. You are that arc or ray of reflective light that allows those attracted to the Light to come out from hiding and step into His presence. You are His stream of light into the darkness. Make sure you stay plugged in to Him and charged with His light by fellowshipping with His saints because it is way too easy to grow used to the hiding place of a little light and that is where the dust and dirt of sin will settle calling to all vermin of darkness to come to this corner to dwell. Free yourself from beginning to flicker and go out by wrapping yourself into the powerful led light of His glory by connecting with others today! Come join me at Bethel Assembly at 10am. Get in church. Shine your light as a reflection of His glory.

The Word was first,
the Word present to God,
God present to the Word.
The Word was God,
in readiness for God from day one.
Everything was created through him;
nothing—not one thing!—
came into being without him.
What came into existence was Life,
and the Life was Light to live by.
The Life-Light blazed out of the darkness;
the darkness couldn't put it out.

John 1: 1-5

WHAT CAME FIRST?

The question that constantly stumps man. This picture shows the creative beauty of God's creation on an amoeba called a dinoflagellate which charges up in sunshine then lights up the ocean at night which is great for us to see but hard for them as it draws predators so they come close to the shore at night because fewer predators are there in the shallows. You see what looks great to one person from the outside can be a challenge to overcome for the other. Often in my consultations, I have parents read a passage with a jumbled code so they can understand the struggle of reading and I ask them after reading the passage…what happened first in the story? 99% cannot tell me because their attention while reading was on puzzling out the code not on comprehension. The purpose is to show the parents what the struggle to read feels like. In this passage, John (the one that came first, before Jesus' earthly birth, as his cousin, son to Elizabeth-who leaped in the womb when he heard Mary was with child)…is telling us the answer to the age-old question. Who came first? The Word. God spoke the words and there was light. God spoke the word and there was all of creation but yet He took the time to form man from the dust and breathe His life into Him. Knowing and experiencing are different. You can know this is a beach because you see the sand, water, palm trees…you can know the dinoflagellates light up the water and have never experienced it. Knowing the Word is God and God is the Word is different than experience.

Understanding the Light of Life and embracing it is like walking into this picture. It's the difference in knowing and KNOWING with understanding and experience. I know a lot of people but very few KNOW me. They think they know me from reading about me, meeting me, knowing my family but KNOWING is deeper. There is an intimacy in understanding that comes when you are experiencing knowledge of a person by walking in a close relationship with them. Do you think that the God Creator of all things doesn't know you? He created you in the innermost place of your mother's womb and brought life. He knows every hair on your head and every tear you shed. He KNOWS you intimately. He Is Alpha and Omega…AtoZ…the beginning to the end…He is first and last. He is yesterday, today and tomorrow. He is your past, your present and your future and He holds you in the palm of His hand. There is nothing that can conquer His light. It blazes out in the deepest oceans and darkest depths of space. He calls light to light and gathers it unto Him and when He gathers all the light unto Himself, the darkness will be complete. In the beginning…God! That's the answer to all. Do you know Him or would you like to KNOW Him? Dive deep into His love. Spend time in His Word because The Word is God. It is light, love and shines in the darkness.

The servant grew up before God—a scrawny seedling,
a scrubby plant in a parched field.
There was nothing attractive about him,
nothing to cause us to take a second look.
He was looked down on and passed over,
a man who suffered, who knew pain firsthand.
One look at him and people turned away.
We looked down on him, thought he was scum.
But the fact is, it was our pains he carried—
our disfigurements, all the things wrong with us.
We thought he brought it on himself,
that God was punishing him for his own failures.
But it was our sins that did that to him,
that ripped and tore and crushed him—our sins!
He took the punishment, and that made us whole.
Through his bruises we get healed.
We're all like sheep who've wandered off and gotten lost.
We've all done our own thing, gone our own way.
And God has piled all our sins, everything we've done
wrong, on him, on him.

Isaiah 53: 2-6

THE CONTRIBUTION!

As I sit here pondering the Word, I hear the chainsaw as Wes cuts trees that are blocking the sunlight on his garden. He has worked that soil, tilled, planted, nourished and watered but he still needed the sunlight to give the plants the best opportunity for growth so that they can produce good fruit. He asked me to go look at his garden the other day and I saw only dirt with a few sprigs of green as I looked through natural eyes. There's nothing attractive about it. This morning it struck me that I am looking carelessly at his work and effort just as many of us have moved past the Easter moment back into our daily routines. We paused to celebrate and have hunts and parties but we moved past it into carelessness less than a week later. The spirit of sin, lawlessness and self has caught our attention again and we look down our noses at His effort as a moment passed. It was this very attitude that dwelled in the people who cheered and sang Hosanna on Palm Sunday as He rode into Jerusalem and a few days later screamed to lose a murderer and crucify Christ. It was our sins that He bore, our selfishness that crushed Him and our willfulness that caused His stripes. Truly this scripture is correct. We are like sheep...all about ourselves, wandering from meal to meal and waterhole to stream to get our fill. I look around me at the beauty of my yard this time of year. It is nothing of my own making.

Wes did all the hard work and just as his garden, a few months ago the yard was bare and not fruitful but now because of his care, it is exploding in color, fragrance and flowers everywhere. It is a masterpiece because he sacrificed his time and effort into it when it was nothing but trouble. Jesus sacrificed his own life for us when we were yet sinners. He knew we would go our own way and yet...He was willing to do the necessary to bring us the opportunity to have eternal life. The work has been done on the cross. The price has been paid. It is time to put off the natural selfishness and lay down the skepticism and willfulness. It is time to take a look at that scrubby seedling and see the sacrifice made for you. I know in a few months that Wes' garden will feed our family and many others. I know that he will continue to work on it to produce. I think it's time I got out of my selfishness and contributed to the cause, pulled a weed and admired that scrubby seedling that will feed me. Many of us need to do the same in our spiritual lives. It's time to quit sitting and observing the holiday as a pastime and lay down our selfishness to follow The Shepherd. Wait, what is that I hear...softly and tenderly, Jesus is calling. Calling for you and for me. See at the portals, He's waiting and watching. Calling all sinners "Come Home!" Come Home, Come Home, all who are weary come home...softly and tenderly Jesus is saying, I sacrificed my life for you, will you lay down yours for me?

"Let me give you a new command: Love one another. In the same way I loved you, you love one another. This is how everyone will recognize that you are my disciples—when they see the love you have for each other."

John 13: 34-35

LOVING LOUD!

A few years ago, Dr Fred Lowery led First Baptist Bossier in a Love Loud campaign. The point was for others to see the love of Christ demonstrated in a huge way across our cities. I remember the bumper stickers and I watched the sermon but the real impact that still has ripples is when my landlord decided to love loud and sponsor a child and an adult to go through brain training. Those ripples still have impact because that changed the lives of those two people and their families. You see both had dyslexia and struggled with reading but by giving the gift of learning to read, both now have opportunities in life they never had before. Jesus gave this commandment to love as He had just demonstrated servanthood by washing their feet and telling them of the sacrifice that He was about to make in love. You see He was loving loud when He went to the cross. His words were not the power on that day, His actions were. I've often heard that actions speak louder than words and this is true especially to those who have acts of service as their love language! Jesus was saying that the actions of love identify you as His. My son often has certain mannerisms of my brother that he never knew...but those mannerisms remind me of my brother.

On today's date in 1989, my brother drew his last earthly breaths and then stepped into glory. The evil actions of a person took his earthly life but the love actions of His Heavenly Father giving His son, gave him eternal life. 1 Corinthians 13 describes love in a lot of ways...it suffers long, it is kind...it compares love to hope and faith then says the greatest of these is love. Love is said to conquer all because it was love that conquered death on the cross through the resurrection of Jesus Christ. Today, I challenge you not to live in memory of the person who you lost on this earth but rather to Love Loud towards others in their memory and in the Love of Christ who gave all for you. It wasn't paying for a meal for others that He did but He said when you do this, you entertain angels unaware. When you Love Loud, you demonstrate who you belong to and His mannerisms & characteristics draw others to Him. Today... let others see Jesus in you!

Consider it a sheer gift, friends, when tests and challenges come at you from all sides. You know that under pressure, your faith-life is forced into the open and shows its true colors. So don't try to get out of anything prematurely. Let it do its work so you become mature and well-developed, not deficient in any way.

James 1: 2-4

THE UNSEEN HAND!

Recognizing the hand of God in your life is sometimes a challenge because we allow things to throw us off course like a tornado tossing things around. I love this picture of the Grand Canyon being formed further because it holds the sheer force and majesty of God in one picture. At first glance you see the mighty rainstorm pouring from the sky, then you see the finger of lightning which has a tornado around it and then you see the promise-the rainbow through the storm. Down below you know that the mighty canyon is filled with flowing blue waters as they race along the floor forming the rock with their power but appearing as a still stream. And the son shines on all of it looking on as its reflective principles show the promises in the storm.

The scripture says consider this a gift when these storms of life come to test and try us. It's true, you know. The Grand Canyon wouldn't be such a wonder of the world without these powerful storms forming and changing the hard rocks into beautiful designs of God's handiwork. The storms bring necessary washing and water to the wildlife...it's God bathing them and refreshing them. I wonder what would happen if we could truly embrace the storms of life as useful, knowing that in the storm there is a promise that God is working all things for our good? Perhaps we could begin to fully understand that He is forming us into the masterpiece of His design? Some people I know love the storms and rain as it makes them sleep. I'm not one of them. I get anxious even though it's only rain. My imagination runs wild in the night and I cannot sleep soundly until the storm passes. I pray and sing. I work on things to keep my mind busy but I don't rest during a storm. I think this is the same for life's storms. Some of us are complete in trust and rest allowing the storm to do what it will and another's anxiously try to find a way to avoid the noise and destruction. Yes, storms tear things up. The power of the water falling tears into the fragile flowers, making rivets in the ground and changing the course of the lay of the land through its streams of water not to mention the lightning that burns and winds that tear. Storms of life are the same and they do bring destruction but there is also purpose and promise in them. Paul instructs us to allow the storms of life to work their purpose, knowing confidentially that there is promise during the storms and afterwards, new life. Storms stir up the bottoms of rivers and oceans, change the courses of streams and make new lakes/puddles. These are important because without the storm stagnation occurs which kills off wildlife and growth allowing the course of nature's bacterias and such to bring death to the riverbed.

Storms wash it away and bring freshness and newness but often we are washed downstream into different circumstances that may be harder with deeper waters and complete newness. Perhaps the death or illness of a loved one, that is the storm which changes our course. Paul tells us not to try to get out of our circumstances prematurely as there is purpose. I'm a worker bee. I'm always flitting about trying new flowers and flavors but steadily building the hive and honey. Storms sometimes take me down and make my wings so wet that I cannot fly and must walk carefully among the weeds as I cannot reach the flowers. But that is when I discovered the wildflower and its sweetness. Soon my wings will dry or heal and I will flitter about again at the beautiful roses but in my mind, I will remember the promise even in the darkest & roughest of storms. This is the journey of faith. Embrace the storms for they are forming a good work in you else God would not have allowed them. Remember He calms storms and angry seas. He alone decides your symphony. He placed every star and planet. His finger is guiding that storm to its true purpose in your life. Press into Him.

Scripture reassures us, "No one who trusts God like this—heart and soul—will ever regret it." It's exactly the same no matter what a person's religious background may be: the same God for all of us, acting the same incredibly generous way to everyone who calls out for help. "Everyone who calls, 'Help, God!' gets help."

Romans 10: 11-13

THE FINAL STEP IN A JOURNEY!

This morning I got the news that a sweet friend had made her final journey home a little earlier than we would have liked due to cancer. At first my heart stumbled but then I remembered it was a journey home past all the struggles here. She has no regrets because she completely trusted God. She fought a very hard battle here for years against this evil but she lived with grace out loud. She trusted God and she lived loud! She called on the name of God and she was saved. She trusted Him heart and soul. That's the best someone could ever say about someone else. The crazy thing is that I was her friend through a friend and because of her cancer journey! We were not intimate friends but we were sisters in Christ Jesus. Her passing through made my life a little sweeter because it makes me remember why Heaven is sounding so much sweeter all the time. God didn't call us to this world to just exist but to live loud in His purpose so that those around us would know that He lived within us. Her final journey wasn't joyful for her close friends & family...yet...but when we grasp ahold of that grace and mercy so that we understand this world isn't our home...then we are joy-filled that our loved ones are walking the streets of glory. Sorrow is a human emotion only here on earth. Grasp this! Jesus wept for Lazarus' death before He resurrected him. He too was overcome by this earth bound emotion then He had that stone rolled away and called forth Lazarus from the grave because He is the resurrection! Hold on my child...joy comes in the morning! Weeping only lasts for the night! The darkest hour means dawn is just in sight!

For what if some did not believe? Will their unbelief make the faithfulness of God without effect? Certainly not! Indeed, let God be true but every man a liar. As it is written: "That You may be justified in Your words, And may overcome when You are judged."

for all have sinned and fall short of the glory of God, being justified freely by His grace through the redemption that is in Christ Jesus,

Romans 3: 3-4, 23-24

REFLECTING LIGHT!

The colors of the moon fascinate me. Man has long had his opinion of things stated as fact as science which has been proven incorrect or certainly not accurate. My dad told me when he was in school, they were taught that the moon was simply a ball of dust magnetically held together...then man was sent to the moon and walked on it. However, there are people who still believe that no one has been to the moon. Does this change things? No. Our beliefs and justifications to life do not change who/what God is or does. God is truth. Scripture says Jesus is the Way, the Truth and the Life and no man comes to the Father except through Jesus. All of us are sinners by nature and birth. But God's redemptive grace restores us to His presence and reveals the truth of Jesus in us so we might be saved and have eternal life. God doesn't need us. We need Him. When you justify something, you line it up perfectly...to a measurement of standard that is fixed. Christ Jesus is that standard of measurement for us. His words are our alignment tool. This moon looks pink and it is gorgeous because the atmosphere around it causes the reflection to tinge pink. The moon isn't pink nor yellow nor blue nor red...the moon is the color of a gray rock with reflective properties. God created that moon to reflect the sun in order to give us light by night. God sent His Son to be our Light and we are to be reflecting His ways, His nature and His promises as lights in the darkest of nights caused by sin around us.

Will the unbelief of those around us cause the Son to not be light? No, it can only become more dark if we refuse to reflect His Sonlight. The sun is always there in the sky, shining. The earth turns and rotates moving further away and closer through the seasons. We too do this in our lives. We choose to live close or far from God's ways, truth and life. Our reflection of His glory depends on our walk. Some choose complete outer darkness and others choose to walk in brilliant reflection. Ultimately, the judgment of God is coming and those who choose to walk out away from His grace will be cast into outer darkness with no chance of God's life when they hear the words...depart from me for I never knew you... today it is your choice...walk in His ways, draw close to His warmth, feel His Sonlight reflecting through you as you draw close to Him. Pink...it's a happy color...maybe my reflection of His glory looks happy and pink to those around me or perhaps it is another color? The only thing that matters is no matter what the atmosphere around me tinges the color of my light...the reflection of His Son should be what all see. God, I wanna be just like you. I want to be a reflection of your glory into the darkest nights.

Then the eleven disciples went away into Galilee, to the mountain which Jesus had appointed for them. When they saw Him, they worshiped Him; but some doubted. And Jesus came and spoke to them, saying, "All authority has been given to Me in heaven and on earth. Go therefore and make disciples of all the nations, baptizing them in the name of the Father and of the Son and of the Holy Spirit, teaching them to observe all things that I have commanded you; and lo, I am with you always, even to the end of the age." Amen.

Matthew 28: 16-20

THE WHY!

What is the most important thing Jesus did after being raised from the dead? He charged His disciples with the carrying on of the good news. We miss this. We celebrate that He is Risen but fail to realize the WHY behind the miracle. He spoke to the women at the tomb saying "Do Not Be Afraid but tell my disciples to go to Galilee and I'll meet them there." Obviously, He was from Galilee in His earthly form...so it makes sense to go there to His family...but I love this part...when they saw Him, they worshiped Him; but some doubted. If you read it in other versions, you see that the ways of the world had stolen their faith...but Jesus didn't speak to this doubt at this time...He charged them. He said ALL authority has been given to me in heaven and on earth. Before His death & resurrection, He functioned within the bounds of earthly authority performing miracles through His Father's name but now...He has surpassed those bounds and is given ALL authority. And with that authority, He charges His disciples, even those who doubted with going out to reach others...teaching, baptizing, and dwelling in Him. With that authority, He charges all of us...even to the end of the age saying that He is with us. Grasp this! Today is a day to celebrate the miracle of life over death but also to realize that Jesus who was given ALL authority charges you with teaching, baptizing and dwelling in His authority. What does this mean? Sickness can't stay any longer, His perfect love casts out all fear. He is the God of all power and it is His will that you be healed.

It is time, church to rise up and begin to operate in the bounds of spiritual freedom and ALL authority over the evil in this world through Jesus' name. He has charged us, called us, empowered us to be His disciples Disciplined in His authority and walking in His freedom. How do you find this authentic authority in Him? Through worship. Worship is the place past the doubt. Worship is the way to overcome the doubt, the fear, the indecision and feelings of lack for in worship, we are charged with His authority over ALL! Through worship, the King of all Kings bestows His power through us from the Heavenliest to the Earth. Today, as you celebrate His resurrection and LIFE, remember He has charged you with ALL authority in Heaven and Earth to reach past the bounds of Earthly principles to the place of miracles. The Miracle of conquering death, hell and the grave to Eternal Life is The Blessed Hope of the Bride. He LIVES! He is coming back! Today may be the day He returns but for sure it is the day of miracles because He Lives!

Still, it's what God had in mind all along,
to crush him with pain. The plan was that he give
himself as an offering for sin so that he'd see life come
from it—life, life, and more life. And God's plan will
deeply prosper through him. Out of that terrible travail
of soul, he'll see that it's worth it and be glad he did it.
Through what he experienced, my righteous one, my
servant, will make many "righteous ones,"
as he himself carries the burden of their sins.
Therefore I'll reward him extravagantly—
the best of everything, the highest honors—
Because he looked death in the face and didn't flinch,
because he embraced the company of the lowest. He
took on his own shoulders the sin of the many, he took
up the cause of all the black sheep.

Isaiah 53: 10-12

THE WEIGHTY PLAN!

Isaiah 53 describes the crucifixion before it occurs...the foreshadowing revealed to the prophet many years prior...on these days when the night seems long and the pain intense, it comforts me greatly to know He has a plan. The simple sentence…Still, it's what God had in mind all along...and God's plan will deeply prosper through Him. You see He knew me in all my weaknesses and yet He loved me. He left glory to endure the suffering and pain even to death on the cross for me and you. Even though Jesus told his disciples who walked with Him exactly what would happen, they doubted, they fretted, they mourned. They saw the weight of all our sins put on Him who knew no sin and they thought...no one can bear that. No one should endure that. Next they'll come for me. And that fleshly concern for self lifted its head and they began to deny Him, hide behind others and huddle in shame. Their hope was broken as He was nailed to the cross because it wasn't possible...but on the darkest day...the celebration of the day of passover when the death angel went house to house claiming the eldest child...the day the only son of God was sacrificed, the curse of death was broken once and for all for believers. The curse caused by man's selfish disobedience is laid to waste by the blood of the Lamb and our testimony. Jesus conquered death, hell & the grave so that when we get to the end of our journey here and it seems all hope is gone... we can remember that He won! Today as we sit in quiet anticipation of tomorrow's celebrations of life... let us remember that God had all of what you are going through in His mind all along. He isn't caught by surprise. His plan is to deeply prosper you if you are willing to take up your cross and follow Him. Trading sin for eternal life...it's His plan and has been all along.

Jesus said, "You're not listening. Let me say it again. Unless a person submits to this original creation—the 'wind-hovering-over-the-water' creation, the invisible moving the visible, a baptism into a new life—it's not possible to enter God's kingdom. When you look at a baby, it's just that: a body you can look at and touch. But the person who takes shape within is formed by something you can't see and touch—the Spirit—and becomes a living spirit.

"So don't be so surprised when I tell you that you have to be 'born from above'—out of this world, so to speak. You know well enough how the wind blows this way and that. You hear it rustling through the trees, but you have no idea where it comes from or where it's headed next. That's the way it is with everyone 'born from above' by the wind of God, the Spirit of God."

John 3: 5-8

YOU'RE NOT LISTENING!

Lately the weather has been quite unpredictable although stormy weather is common for this time of year for sure. In this passage Jesus is explaining the unexplainable to Nicodemus and he just cannot grasp what is being said. I love this particular version for its plain speaking manner. Jesus explains here that entering into God's kingdom requires rebirth but not of the natural...of the spirit. He is speaking about the state of the spiritual soul of man. The invisible that moves the visible. We hear thunder and we see lightning, we feel the wind and we can see, hear, feel, smell and taste the rain...yet we don't understand all that is behind the weather. I teasingly say that a meteorologist is the only job where you can get your job wrong and still have a job because we understand that weather is not controlled by man but rather the invisible controlling the visible. Jesus compares our spiritual souls to this wind. Moved by the unseen into doing the seen. But He clearly says...You're not listening...unless you submit to this original creation...meaning the moving of the Spirit of God within the soul-you cannot enter Heaven...God's kingdom.

We cannot know exactly when a tornado will strike although we may see indications of it on radar and know enough to predict the possibility of one...the actual event is uncontrollable and unpredictable. This uncertainty of things vexes the spirit of man but in rebirth, there is peace in the storm. Storms of life both literally and figuratively are not always within our purview but our reaction-the peace within the storm is like the eye of the hurricane...although the storm rages around it...the eye is still and completely calm. God created each of us both in the natural and the supernatural. Our very soul is His and that longing to belong comes from Him. When we allow the invisible hand of God to have reign in our lives, the invisible controls the visible and we have peace, hope and security. Today is a day of reckoning as we look back at how man, once again, tried to control the unknown and uncontrollable Spirit of God within a man called Jesus. Jesus chose the way of the cross to conquer death, hell and the grave once and for all with a completely pure sacrifice of Himself. Sin is defeated through His sacrifice but we must choose to accept this gift of life eternal by a rebirth into the original spirit of creation. We must get back to where He designed us to live...an immortal being encased in mortal flesh. We must begin to see the invisible spiritual world for what it is and quit walking as if this mortality is our existence. Today, as Jesus gave up the Spirit into the keeping of the Father, the religious veil in the temple was rent in half...the veil that separated us from the spirit is gone if we, but yield to Him. You see the evidence of the wind but fail to understand it just as you see the evidence of God and fail to grasp Him. His love is like a tornado ripping through this world, tearing at the fabric of the veil that shields the known from the unknown. His love is calling to you to submit to Him so He can make the invisible more visible in your life. Today is Good Friday...it's good because He chose the way of the cross for you... The choice is yours. Will you be born out of this world into His spirit? Will you exchange the mortal for immortality??

Today His love is calling...will you listen?

When Jesus was at Bethany, a guest of Simon the Leper, a woman came up to him as he was eating dinner and anointed him with a bottle of very expensive perfume. When the disciples saw what was happening, they were furious. "That's criminal! This could have been sold for a lot and the money handed out to the poor."

When Jesus realized what was going on, he intervened. "Why are you giving this woman a hard time? She has just done something wonderfully significant for me. You will have the poor with you every day for the rest of your lives, but not me. When she poured this perfume on my body, what she really did was anoint me for burial. You can be sure that wherever in the whole world the Message is preached, what she has just done is going to be remembered and admired."

That is when one of the Twelve, the one named Judas Iscariot, went to the cabal of high priests and said, "What will you give me if I hand him over to you?" They settled on thirty silver pieces. He began looking for just the right moment to hand him over.

Matthew 26: 6-16

THE COST OF OIL!

It strikes me that as we look at this scripture, the disciples are aware that the time with Jesus is short...he's already told them this...they are eating at the house of a leper that Jesus healed...a place of reminder of His power and yet...when this woman came in to follow her heart's leading, the verse says "they were furious". They were angry that someone had "wasted" what they could've sold for money. This was the "church" who had experienced every miracle from walking on water to the lame walking, blind seeing, lepers miraculously healed...and yet Money was the reason for the betrayal then as it often is now. Jesus tells them to stop and explains why this is such an important act and yet...this is the moment Judas decides on betrayal. Money and concern about it is often a claw in families, marriages, relationships and even leads to murder. Scripture tells us that the love of money (security) is often the one thing that trumps our relationship with God...it even tells us that it is harder for a rich man to go to Heaven than a camel to go through the eye of a needle. Why? Because we sacrifice ourselves for the dollar and security. We put our jobs before God. We put our welfare before God. We trust in the dollar before we trust in God. Today, on this day of reflection...the day that a woman poured her special gift worth its weight in gold at the Master's feet...I ask you...what is the cost of the oil in your Alabaster box? Are you willing to pour it out at Jesus' feet or has it become more important to you than His sacrifice...His life...His salvation from the wages of sin? What is the cost of your praise? You offer it up at your child's ball games easily and even pay to go scream at the top of your lungs for people you don't even know...is His life enough to pay for your praise? Are you willing to sacrifice your time, your money, your self importance for Him? What is the cost of the oil in your alabaster box?

Since Jesus went through everything you're going through and more, learn to think like him. Think of your sufferings as a weaning from that old sinful habit of always expecting to get your own way. Then you'll be able to live out your days free to pursue what God wants instead of being tyrannized by what you want.

Friends, when life gets really difficult, don't jump to the conclusion that God isn't on the job. Instead, be glad that you are in the very thick of what Christ experienced. This is a spiritual refining process, with glory just around the corner.

If you're abused because of Christ, count yourself fortunate. It's the Spirit of God and his glory in you that brought you to the notice of others. If they're on you because you broke the law or disturbed the peace, that's a different matter. But if it's because you're a Christian, don't give it a second thought. Be proud of the distinguished status reflected in that name!

1 Peter 4: 1-2, 12-16

WEANING FROM TYRANNY!

Selfishness is tyranny of your own life. Suffering is really a weaning from the sinful habit of getting our own way in things. Freedom comes from the spiritual refining process which releases us from the tyranny of selfishness. The point here is that if we change our mindset to see that stress, problems and circumstances of our own making can be used to refine us into freedom...then we could get out from under the tyranny of selfish dependency.

The refining process is necessary to make anything pure and useful from crude oil to water to silver/gold, glass... and us! God must take us through the refining process in order to get us free from the tyranny of self/flesh. We are born into sin which comes with the selfish expectation of getting our own way. From an early age, the world indoctrination of "have it your way" inundates us until we surrender to Christ's freedom which is yielding to His path. But oh, this is the journey to spiritual freedom. Yielding to Him releases us to freedom of dependency on our own selves and the bondage to the tyranny of selfishness. You see, our ways aren't God's ways. I hear so often...if God was really love...He would...or wouldn't...this is the tyranny mindset of man trying to control circumstances around him by boxing God into the selfishness mindset. We are not mini gods or demigods. We are His people. We are to be yielded to Him fully. Refining processes involve heat, pressure & time. The higher the heat and pressure, the less time it takes to make a diamond from a piece of coal. Man has mimicked making diamonds and these are called cubic zirconias...but the shortened process while making a beautiful stone still doesn't make the same quality as the diamond that has gone through the God process.

I'm saying this for you to understand that no matter how eager you are to rush through your situation and find a quick answer/solution...you are trying to inject the tyranny of man's mindedness on God and it will not happen! This Cain/Ishmael/Esau mindset is abhorrent to God. When man tries to inject his tyranny of selfishness to rush the refining process... you get the weight of the sin. Jesus came and walked out the process to the point of death on the cross to show us that we must sacrifice this mindset to grow into what he has for us...this refining is not easy. In fact, it's trying and hard. It is intense, long and overwhelming but it is freedom when you begin to accept the refining as His work. You escape the mortal bounds and understand true freedom isn't in this but only in Him. A caterpillar must go into a cocoon and be refined to escape the current status and emerge as a butterfly. A seed must die to become a plant that has fruit. Our selfishness must be yielded to be refined. The heat of circumstances and pressures of life are given to us as a gift of refinement. Catch the mindset to be like Jesus. Wean yourself from the tyranny of selfishness by leaning into His ways. Acknowledge Him in all your ways and He will direct your path. Lord, make me a vessel. Make me an offering. Make me whatever you want me to be. I came here with nothing and all that you've given me...Jesus, crush my selfishness like grapes are crushed so I may be refined into your glory useful for your purposes.

"Let me give you a new command: Love one another. In the same way I loved you, you love one another. This is how everyone will recognize that you are my disciples—when they see the love you have for each other."

John 13: 34-35

REFLECTION!

Most people can look up into the sky and recognize the moon even if it is still showing in the daytime. One young lady took the time to photograph the moon everyday for a month from the exact same physical location and as the earth moved, the moon's position is changed in the photos...probably would form a eternity knot if she kept going...It has different stages as shown in the pictures and different colors but we clearly know it is the moon. The moon only gets its light by reflection of the light of the sun. This is exactly what Jesus is saying in this scripture...we are put here for the purpose of reflection of His Love. If His love is reflected in our lives no matter what stage of walk we are in growth in Him, people will recognize us for who we belong to and know Him. The moon reflects the sun. We are to reflect The Son. In pure reflection, you may see different colors of this love from working together in love until reaching out to others in His love, like the rays of the sun reflecting onto the moon to shed light into the darkness, shines onto us so we may reflect His Sonlight into the darkness of this world. No matter what stage of life you are in or what's happening, God's love is shining through the light of His Son and you are called to be this light-this reflection of His love into the darkest part of the world...into your workplace, your home, your world. Only you can touch these lives with the light of His love in this way. You are called to be His reflection. Lord, let my life touch a heart that hurts today. Help me to reflect your light of love in all that I do today.

Think of yourselves the way Christ Jesus thought of himself. He had equal status with God but didn't think so much of himself that he had to cling to the advantages of that status no matter what. Not at all. When the time came, he set aside the privileges of deity and took on the status of a slave, became human! Having become human, he stayed human. It was an incredibly humbling process. He didn't claim special privileges. Instead, he lived a selfless, obedient life and then died a selfless, obedient death—and the worst kind of death at that—a crucifixion.

Because of that obedience, God lifted him high and honored him far beyond anyone or anything, ever, so that all created beings in heaven and on earth—even those long ago dead and buried—will bow in worship before this Jesus Christ, and call out in praise that he is the Master of all, to the glorious honor of God the Father.

Philippians 2: 5-11

LET THIS MIND BE IN YOU!

He humbled himself and became obedient to the point of His death on the cross...therefore God exalted Him that His name is above every name. This picture is of Elephant Island in Ireland. It truly looks like a sleeping mama elephant...down to the details on the rocks but from above for sure. When I first saw it, I thought it was a picture of a sleeping elephant except it had a lot of green. The point here is form. The rocks/island are in the form of an elephant but this is not really an elephant. Jesus took on the form of man and although He was God...He chose obedience. He did not get crucified by man but chose to humble himself for our salvation to the point of death so that He might once again conquer through His sacrifice and His resurrection! The scripture says it all...we should allow this mindset to become ours...humbleness and obedience. You see these are the hardest for us as humans. From the moment a child is born, the sin nature screams for its own desires and needs. It demands these to be satisfied immediately. It was one of the hardest things I've ever done to instruct that screaming & crying baby into a sleep/eat schedule by "ignoring" the cry (there really is no ignoring happening, more like endurance training for me). This was an important part of them learning obedience but terribly hard. No one wants to punish their child but obedience takes training and the sin nature abhors anything that limits its getting its way. Jesus wept tears of blood and sweated blood as he prayed before He was able to humble His sin nature into obedience and He was God incarnate. My point here is that humbleness and obedience like love is a constant choice. Not a one and done. You must choose each time when that sin nature rises to submit to God's will rather than your own and to humble yourself to His will. Jesus prayed not my will but thine Lord. This is what led God to exalt His name above all others that at the name of Jesus everything and everyone in earth and above/beyond must bow down. This mindset of humility and obedience led to exultation but that's not what His motive was...His motivation was you. He desired to make a way for you, an example for you. He grew the tree that He knew would be used to make the old rugged cross. Nothing took His life, but with love He gave it. Such great love for you that Jesus followed God's perfect plan in humble obedience. Now, He has given you a path of self sacrifice in humble obedience to follow. Knowing He has promised you exultation and an eternal hope of life everlasting... knowing He did it for you...are you willing to lay down yourself so that another may come to know Him through your humble obedience? Are you willing to lay down your pride and your ways to hear His voice guiding you into His reality? Are you willing to stand out and be counted as His before others? Are you willing to be known for Association as His child? Think on it. Isn't today the day to choose the mindset of humble obedience? Lord, paint my mind with Calvary's blood so that I may live and walk in humble obedience to you. Use me Lord to draw one to you today.

The disciples began to rejoice and praise God with a loud voice for all the mighty works they had seen, saying:" 'Blessed is the King who comes in the name of the Lord!' Peace in heaven and glory in the highest!"

But He answered and said to them, "I tell you that if these should keep silent, the stones would immediately cry out."

Luke 19: 38,40

THE DIVIDED!

My heart has been so heavy this morning because God showed me the divided mind of the church through this today. I am still mulling on it with a broken heart. The "church" has sold its relationship with God for a few pieces of silver and He is about to judge her by taking only his pure bride, who resides in relationship with Him daily, home. The rest will be left to repent their ways through a turbulent time. Oh that we would draw so close as His time is drawing near. Please my loved ones... please...repent and draw near. He's waiting for you & me to draw closer.

You see it was The Pharisees, the highest of the church, the most devoted to the law that refused to acknowledge Him as Lord. Are we so caught up in our world, our work, our government and our rules that we too fail to recognize Him? Only His bride walking in relationship with Him will hear His call to come away in the Rapture of the Church. Only His bride...His true bride who is spotless and without wrinkle...the time has come to press in. His anointing is flowing and it is time that we trust as we have never trusted before. It is time we look only to Him for the way is about to become extremely rocky and then He comes. All nature is set to scream at the top of her lungs to His glory as many of those He sacrificed and died for have turned their backs on Him. Prepare you the way. If today was The Day...what would you do? Who would you reach out to? Why are you waiting?

Lift up your heads, O you gates!
And be lifted up, you everlasting doors!
And the King of glory shall come in.
Who is this King of glory?
The Lord strong and mighty,
The Lord mighty in battle.
Lift up your heads, O you gates!
Lift up, you everlasting doors!
And the King of glory shall come in.
Who is this King of glory?
The Lord of hosts,
He is the King of glory.

Psalms 24: 7-10

LIFT UP YOUR HEAD!

I will confess that I had a really hard morning and my heart was hurting badly until I turned to the scripture and heard My Father say Lift up your head! He's so good to provide just the words I needed! He is my defense and my shield when I fear. He is my God who is mighty in battle no matter what the war that's raging.

He is my King, my confidence and my confidante. I sit here in my car reflecting on His words and looking at the pure beauty of His creation around me at this beautiful place... I know that God will fight my battles.

Offer the sacrifices of righteousness, And put your trust in the Lord. There are many who say, "Who will show us any good?" Lord, lift up the light of Your countenance upon us. You have put gladness in my heart, More than in the season that their grain and wine increased.

I will both lie down in peace, and sleep; For You alone, O Lord, make me dwell in safety.

Psalms 4:5-8

PROJECT AND REFLECT!

My talented friend Rajeesh shared this recent photo he took. It is a reflection of the heavens in the waters below. It is the light of God's glory on the water in the picture and I couldn't help but wonder how the Light of His countenance reflects in me. He puts gladness in my heart when by the world's standards I don't have enough to be glad about. He gives me peace to sleep in the midst of the storm knowing that no matter what happens, I am safe in Him. Why? Because I put my trust in Him and offer the sacrifices of righteousness even when things are tough. Here's some toe stepping...recently several people posted their opinion about getting drunk and saying that it was an okay Christian thing to do because Jesus turned water into wine at a wedding for His first miracle. My only response to this is "how were you shining the light of Jesus while you were acting like the devil?" I choose not to ever overindulge my flesh with things of the flesh because that is a path to destruction. Does this make me perfect? No...it means I am offering the sacrifices of righteousness. I love me some chocolate and I love other things to eat and enjoy but I do not (despite how I look) overindulge because it is detrimental to my health and I am the temple of God. I choose not to imbibe alcohol ever as in I have never ever had a single drop because I trust God and this is a personal conviction. I know people who drink and I leave that to them and their relationship with God.

Alcohol is like any other addictive drug...it has consequences and they are painful. I have seen so many who have gotten addicted to pornography or pain pills or iPhones or novels or...addiction is a trap, a chain, a prison of the mind, body, heart, etc. It starts easily and is reflected in your life onto your kids, your family, your friends, etc. It has a terrible ripple effect that goes on and on and that disturbs the reflection of God's countenance in your life. So let me ask again, who or what are you reflecting today? A God of peace because you trust Him over your finances and other problems as you strive to walk in His countenance or are you walking in the mud reflecting nothing but the muck you are bound by? Isn't it time you examined yourself and made a choice. I choose gladness over fame and health over wealth. I choose righteousness over social popularity. I choose love and sacrifice over power because my God has supplied me with all I need according to His riches in glory. Who will show "us" any good?...God's countenance reflecting into the pools of the lives of His people. Go project/reflect His light, His countenance, His goodness and His gladness into the lives of those around you.

But what happens when we live God's way? He brings gifts into our lives, much the same way that fruit appears in an orchard—things like affection for others, exuberance about life, serenity. We develop a willingness to stick with things, a sense of compassion in the heart, and a conviction that a basic holiness permeates things and people. We find our-selves involved in loyal commitments, not needing to force our way in life, able to marshal and direct our energies wisely. Legalism is helpless in bringing this about; it only gets in the way. Among those who belong to Christ, everything connected with getting our own way and mindlessly responding to what everyone else calls necessities is killed off for good—crucified. Since this is the kind of life we have chosen, the life of the Spirit, let us make sure that we do not just hold it as an idea in our heads or a sentiment in our hearts, but work out its implications in every detail of our lives. That means we will not compare ourselves with each other as if one of us were better and another worse. We have far more interesting things to do with our lives. Each of us is an original.

Galatians 5: 22-26 MSG

But the fruit of the Spirit is love, joy, peace, long suffering, kindness, goodness, faithfulness, gentleness, self-control. Against such there is no law. And those who are Christ's have crucified the flesh with its passions and desires. If we live in the Spirit, let us also walk in the Spirit. Let us not become conceited, provoking one another, envying one another.

Galatians 5: 22-26 NKJV

FRUITFUL BOWELS!

"Don't get your bowels in an uproar" is my dad's favorite saying when we try to hurry him along in something. I know he means to quit pushing him and take time but I never truly got the meaning until my guts literally were in an uproar for a year in 2018 resulting in a bowel resection. When I went for a follow up, the doctor's instructions were to eat an apple or a pear everyday! I know "an apple a day keeps the doctor away" and it works...the fiber makes things run smoothly. Now why...well, let's dive into what Paul is instructing the church at Galatia. He is admonishing them to bear fruit of the Spirit of God and not the bad fruit of the flesh. You see it is much easier and more convenient to take shortcuts in our lives. I mean taking a fiber pill accomplishes the same thing as eating fruit right? Technically it is fiber but you miss out on the other things the body needs. Eating fruit wasn't just about the fruit, it is about encouraging healthy habits instead of convenience and shortcuts. We all love convenience and microwaves are nice but a home cooked meal just tastes like love and everyone I know enjoys that. My point is that we often get so hyper focused on the fruit of the spirit that we forget the rest. I put two versions of this scripture here because I want you to read both and think on both. Having the fruit of the Spirit actively producing in your life requires the sacrifice of self and the laying down of your own passions and desires in exchange for His. It is so easy to get caught up in the political fray about everything but is that producing fruit? It's how you act in times of stress that demonstrates your fruit. Are you demonstrating love, peace, gentleness, kindness?...against these there are no laws...people like this kind of fruit...it's tasty and attractive and pleasant and digestible. In these times of uncertainty and stress and the unknown, what kind of example are you? Are you selflessly leading others or is the true fruit seeping out into the world around with a rotting smell?

Did your convenient word of the day or scripture of the day last or is it festering and rotting undigested? I'm not trying to be disgusting here but I am trying to get you to understand that there are no shortcuts to diving deep into a relationship with God. It is just you that is affected by your choice but the ripple effect of sweet fruit or rotting fruit is huge. I'm trying to help those of you with overripe bananas in your life to make some banana pudding instead of letting that fruit sit there and rot. It is time to take a real look into your fruit basket that you are...are you producing the fruits that draw people or are you just drawing fruit flies as you rot? Lord, help me to be fruitful and multiply. Help me to produce fruit in my life that attracts others to your glory. When I get into places where I refuse to take the time to digest and instead rush for convenience, help direct me into a place of obedience and fruitfulness.

Christ arrives right on time to make this happen. He didn't, and doesn't, wait for us to get ready. He presented himself for this sacrificial death when we were far too weak and rebellious to do anything to get ourselves ready. And even if we hadn't been so weak, we wouldn't have known what to do any way we can understand someone dying for a person worth dying for, and we can understand how someone good and noble could inspire us to selfless sacrifice. But God put his love on the line for us by offering his Son in sacrificial death while we were of no use whatever to him.

Romans 5: 6-8

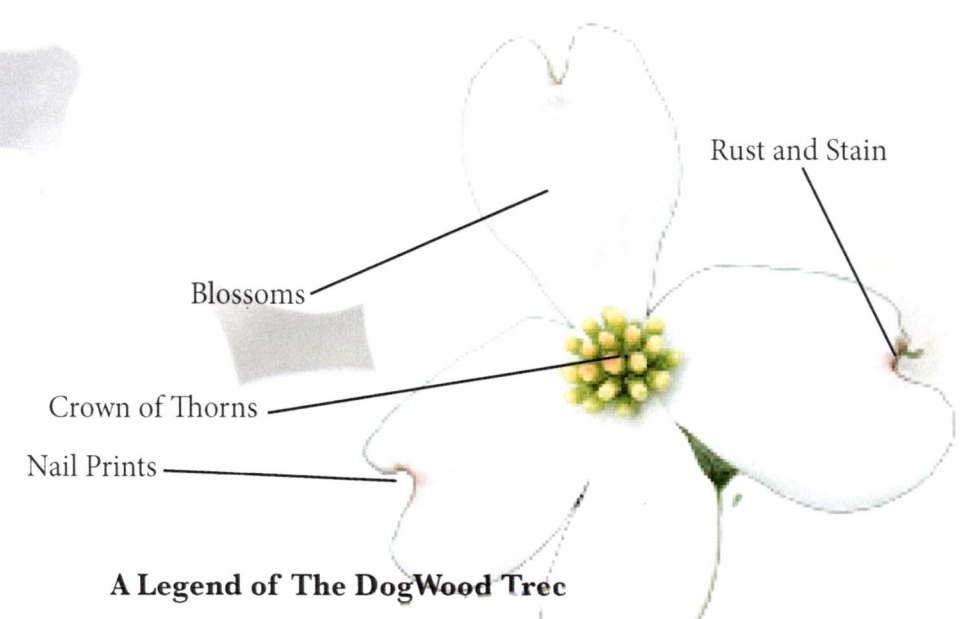

Rust and Stain

Blossoms

Crown of Thorns

Nail Prints

A Legend of The DogWood Tree

When Christ was on earth, the dogwood grew; to a towering size with a lovely hue. It's branches were strong and interwoven and for Christ's cross its timbers were chosen.

Being distressed at the use of the wood, Christ made a promise which still holds good.

"Not ever again shall the dogwood grow to be large enough for such a tree and so slender and twisted it shall always be with cross-shaped blossoms for all to see. The petals shall have bloodstains marked in brown and in the all blossom's center a thorny crown. All who see it shall think of me nailed to a cross from a dogwood tree. Protected and cherished the tree shall be a reflection to all of my agony."

WOULD YOU DIE FOR ME?

The truth hurts but the answer of truth for most is no. I think we would say yes as a knee jerk response but when it truly comes to that moment of laying it down, most of us would cave. I have always been fascinated with the Legend of the Dogwood tree. It's a beautiful thought that a tree still carries the crucifixion of my Savior in its innermost being and produces a replication of its symbolism in its petals. What a beautiful thought! The representation of Christ's sacrifice for me in that before I was even born, before my parents or my grandparents or even my great, great, great grandparents were born...Jesus Christ, the King of Glory came as a baby, dwelt here on Earth for 33 plus years and then laid down His life for me. It wasn't easy for Him either. In the Garden of Gethsemane, Jesus was under such a battle in his prayer time that He wept tears of blood. You see His battle wasn't on the day of crucifixion...that was just the carrying through...the battle was won in the Garden in prayer.

So back to my question..,would you die for me? Further, would you sacrifice your son for me? I watched my parents lose their eldest son and the sorrow we all felt. We are changed for life. Every April we mourn him. Every April, we realize that he isn't here and he would have had a passel of kids and probably grandkids by now knowing Micah Drew. I see him in my sons and I think of him often in my heart/mind. Would I give up my brother for you? Would I give up my son for you? Would I give up my own life for you? Truly, I don't think I would as much as I care. I want to say yes because I do care but the truth is I want to ask questions like what are you going to do with the life I give you? Is it going to be more than the value received by the life it is exchanged for in that moment?

This is what God did. He gave His son. Jesus gave His own life for you while you were still too busy to acknowledge Him. He sacrificed it all for you to live eternally, to fight back against death, hell & the grave. No greater love has there ever been than this. No greater love will there ever be.

So my final question...what are you doing with the life that God sacrificed His own son for? That Jesus wept tears of blood & died a horrendous death on a cross for? Maybe the dogwood tree was the sacrificial tree and it forever changed and bleeds red when it is cut because it remembers the Lord's death. Maybe that is how the dogwood tree demonstrates its love for its creator. What are you doing about Jesus' sacrifice? 🎼 Who am I that a king would bleed and die for? Who am I that He would pray not my will but thine for? The answer I may never know why He ever loved me so but to the old rugged cross he bore for you and I.

This Book of the Law shall not depart from your mouth, but you shall meditate in it day and night, that you may observe to do according to all that is written in it. For then you will make your way prosperous, and then you will have good success. Have I not commanded you? Be strong and of good courage; do not be afraid, nor be dismayed, for the Lord your God is with you wherever you go."

Joshua 1: 8-9

THE DRIVE!

Prosperity and Success are two things that drive the human race. Some people seek fame and power as the means to get these and they invest all of themselves into the path that forces others into their molds in order to achieve and yet they are not happy...they are desperate, fearful and hungry. If you look at the current political climate and most of the media, this is what you will see. I hurt for them as they are so lost. They missed the key instructions and they operate in fear and dismay. The people of Israel were in this place of slavery in Egypt with the hands of Pharaoh around their necks but God chose a mom willing to stand out against the norm and risk her life for her child. She doesn't get a lot of acclaim because she fades into the background of the story but Moses' mom believed God. She watched God move in her life and that of her children and she taught them these principles before there were any books of Law...as these Moses wrote. When God speaks to Joshua in these verses, He has already worked many miracles that Joshua has seen. He has already sent many examples before Joshua including Moses who has just died and He is charging Joshua with carrying forward His purpose. Sometimes we look around us and all that has gone before us is changed. We don't recognize our new landscape and suddenly those who were our examples aren't there. But God gave Moses His law, His guide, His commandments and Moses recorded them. God instructed Joshua to meditate on them day and night...Get them inside his heart and mind so he could do all they directed him to do for they were and are the keys to success. Prosperity comes from a place of security and success from a place of confidence. This is why God told Joshua to be strong and of good courage confident that God was with him. Fear undermines success and dismay overwhelms confidence.

If you operate outside the boundaries of God's laws, heaping upon yourself and seeking fame/fortune at the cost of others, you live in constant fear and jeopardy of losing everything because it's all false. Dwelling in the place of strength and courage requires confidence in who He is and to do this you must meditate in His word so that it diffuses into your very being. Prosperity and success come from understanding that He is your all. There is nothing that man can take from you because all that you value is in Him. My hope is in you Lord, my strength is in you Lord, my life is in you Lord. My joy is in you Lord, my successes are in you Lord, my walk and my purpose are in you. I will praise you all of my days. I will love you all my life. With all that I am, I will meditate in you so that I may find my success and my prosperity in you. Thank you for your secret way...the way of strength and courage in the face of fear and defeat. I am so grateful that I have known you all of my days. Go before me as my sun and my shield. Give me strength and guide me in your glory. For you oh God are my life wherever I am.

Light, space, zest—
that's God!
So, with him on my side I'm fearless,
afraid of no one and nothing.

I'm asking God for one thing,
only one thing:
To live with him in his house
my whole life long.
I'll contemplate his beauty;
I'll study at his feet.
That's the only quiet, secure place
in a noisy world,
The perfect getaway,

far from the buzz of traffic.

Psalms 27: 1, 4-5

IN THE QUIET!

Today has been a very hectic day and yet...I feel full of His glory. I contemplate him all day long in my waking and sleeping. This is my quiet in the midst of the rush. I breathe Him in, dwell in Him and delight in Him. Zest is the perfect word. It's a joie de vivre...a joy of life...knowing that I am His and He is mine. Do I get overwhelmed? Sure I do, when I forget to dwell in Him and begin to look at the hustle and bustle. Stop, breathe Him in. Feel His light, His space as He expands within you. Focus on Him and allow His zest to fill you...just take a minute...picture Him high on this mountaintop waiting to see you...then allow yourself to take it in. Study at His feet. Contemplate His beauty. Then you'll dwell with Him in His house instead of the buzzing noise of this world. Thank you Lord for your quiet, your peace, your calm.

My physical therapist tells me to breathe all the time because it does calm the mind and allow you to feel yourself. It also allows you to hear Him in that still small voice. Better is one day in His house than a thousand elsewhere.

As soon as Peter and John were let go, they went to their friends and told them what the high priests and religious leaders had said. Hearing the report, they lifted their voices in a wonderful harmony in prayer: "Strong God, you made heaven and earth and sea and everything in them. By the Holy Spirit you spoke through the mouth of your servant and our father, David:

Why the big noise, nations?
Why the mean plots, peoples?
Earth's leaders push for position,
Potentates meet for summit talks,
The God-deniers, the Messiah-defiers!

"And now they're at it again! Take care of their threats and give your servants fearless confidence in preaching your Message, as you stretch out your hand to us in healings and miracles and wonders done in the name of your holy servant Jesus."

While they were praying, the place where they were meeting trembled and shook. They were all filled with the Holy Spirit and continued to speak God's Word with fearless confidence.

Acts 4: 23-26, 29-30

DRY BONES!

Stretch out your hand, Lord once again, so your people can demonstrate your power once again. Like Samson, we have moved away from your righteousness and have given our authority over to men who used our weaknesses to cripple us. But we your church, your bride have renewed our covenant with you in repentance and ask for you to stretch out your hand again in miracles, powerful wonders and healings in the name above all names Jesus Christ.

Lord, we need a soul deep revival of your Spirit, that which empowered Paul to speak from his chains of bondage with authority. We need a renewing and awakening of your spirit within us so that dry bones start rattling and dead men walk again. Lord, we need your shaking and quaking of the spirits of those who have been the closet warriors to once again rise up and proclaim your sovereignty. We need folks who will stand up for your righteousness for your glory. We need men and women, young and old who will walk openly in your authenticity and authority with no fear for tomorrow or the plans of men. Give us fearless confidence and holy boldness to go forth in our workplace and our everyday life performing miracles in your name, prophesying, leading the souls of men to you, casting out devils and baptizing in the name of the Father, the Son and the Holy Ghost! God, help us to rise up, to press in, to hold close to your unchanging and unwavering hand in these evil times. I pray for fire to fall as it did on the day of Pentecost! I pray for your power to be demonstrated in all the earth today in a mighty way so that others may know and be blessed. I hear your calling. I see your vision. I know you are coming soon and the souls of men are anxious for a magnificent harvest! Revive us O Lord to your work to your reckoning to your purposes to your plans to your heart, your love, your mind. Transform our spirits within us to awaken us to your glory! Hallelujah!

Just as lotions and fragrance give
sensual delight,
a sweet friendship refreshes the soul.
You use steel to sharpen steel,
and one friend sharpens another.
If you care for your orchard, you'll
enjoy its fruit; if you honor your boss,
you'll be honored.
Just as water mirrors your face,
so your face mirrors your heart.

Proverbs 27: 9, 17-19

FRIENDS!

Friends...these verses are about all different types of friends...

I have lots of friends and you all fall into different categories from the FB friend who only knows me through FB to those who are intimately acquainted with me but there is a common thread through all...I care about you and I pray for you! As my housekeeper and close friends know, I have a lot of different lotions and fragrances but strangely enough I don't have a favorite. Each day I select a different one to delight and excite me. This is the way I feel about friends. I have never had that one friend who was my only BFF...unless you count my mom and my husband...I have tons of friends and I am open to each of them. I have special relationships with some that are deeper than with others as time and care grow the roots and sharpens us. There are some people I will readily take admonition from and others I must weigh. There are those I allow to speak into my life intimately and others I choose to stay distant from but still enjoy. There are friends who know my favorite color & food & likes and friends who I am just happy to see. The thing is that friendship is a real product of work. Yesterday I had brunch with a special young lady in my life who I admire and consider a special friend but we haven't seen each other in a year. She's wonderful and special and we are both ok with our relationship continuing in real life time. If someone asked me who my best friend is...well, I have a close friend who I haven't seen in many many years that in my mind holds that place because she was there intimately in my life for a lot of years... we don't talk often nor know much about each other today but my friend is in my heart...she knew me when...my husband and I have close couple friends who have been there through a lot of things and there is an intimacy there that no others know...my point is that friendship is like an orchard that grows fruit and sometimes one tree gets more attention than the others but all still produce with love and care. I like to think my friends mirror me like my face mirrors my heart. I am open to all, pure in my thoughts and intentions to my friends. I want the best for each and every one of you. Some of you I see often, some I do not but I dearly love you all! I pray for you! I think of you and today I bless you. Thank you for your friendship! Thank you for being you! Thank you for writing into my life whether it is a little or a lot. You make me better because I have you as my friends. If we haven't connected in a while, it doesn't mean I don't care...it's just life...it's real. Call me, text me, email me...PM me...let's do lunch or just chat!

Thinking of you makes me smile!

And that about wraps it up. God is strong, and he wants you strong. So take everything the Master has set out for you, well-made weapons of the best materials. And put them to use so you will be able to stand up to everything the Devil throws your way. This is no weekend war that we'll walk away from and forget about in a couple of hours. This is for keeps, a life-or-death fight to the finish against the Devil and all his angels.

Ephesians 6: 10-12

WEAPONS OF WARFARE!

When I was young I visited some civil war battlefields in VA and remarked to my dad that it was serene and looked like any other place. It's true that battlefields are rarely ugly places but rather plain places where people live and breathe. The battle is often taking place right where everyday life takes place. This is true for spiritual battles too. God has prepared you for the battle in your life with all the tools that you need but you must employ them. The first time I picked up a gun, I wasn't familiar with the feel of it or how to use it but I knew I could point and shoot. With practice and familiarity, I'm actually quite a good shot. The same is true with His Word which is a two edged sword piercing into the very bone & sinew...you must practice using it by reading and honing the words so that you can engage them when the battle is fierce. When fear comes, you can swipe it away with "God hasn't given me a spirit of fear but of love and a sound mind". When troubles arise, "no weapon formed against me shall prosper". Jesus himself in the great temptation by the master deceiver used the Sword of the Word...in every temptation He said...The Word says...He was demonstrating the use of The Sword to us. God is well versed in His word as His word is so powerful that it quells storms and creates life. In the beginning was the Word...the Word was with God and The Word was God...He spoke Let there be Light and there was Light...understand that the battlefields, many of our own making, are in our everyday life in our waking and sleeping...in our everyday. But He has said that there is nothing that will come your way that He hasn't already seen and already prepared the tools, weapons, and a way of escape for you.

You have only to employ them. His weapons are powerful...there is nothing stronger than the power of love, joy, peace...all the magic in the world is undone in God's love...everyone is undone in love. Let's not downplay that this is a war for the souls of men and it is a fierce battle with intense weaponry of evil. The devil will come at you with all his arsenal has...but his weapons may look like F16s when they are paper airplanes held together with cobwebs against the word of God. The biggest battlefield is the mind and it is like a spiderweb. The thought comes in like a creepy spider waiting to pounce, weaving its web of deceit and as long as you don't panic and get wrapped up in the web, you can navigate with the power of the word through all the traps and succeed. Walk in His peace and security through uncertainty rather than allowing the panic to wrap you up in the cobwebs of deceit. God has given you the tools. If you know you have a battle ahead, sit down and write His words on your heart by inscribing them on cards that you can pick up and read when the battle is fierce. Hone that weapon. Smooth it, shine it, sharpen it. The battle is happening whether you are ready or not. Best to prepare for each skirmish in advance so that you are not caught unawares. Finally, remember that the battle isn't just taking place in you. You are not alone! He is with you and He calls up others in your time of need to the battle on knees...the battle of prayer. Prayer is powerful for it binds together the many though they may be in different physical locations. The power of prayer has changed many a battlefield into places of celebration. The power of prayer opens doors. So let's employ the armor of God...the whole armor and get busy fighting...for this battle belongs to God and can be fought on my knees.

Up with God!
Down with his enemies!
Adversaries, run for the hills!
Gone like a puff of smoke,
like a blob of wax in the fire—
one look at God and the wicked vanish.
When the righteous see God in
action they'll laugh, they'll sing,
they'll laugh and sing for joy.
Sing hymns to God; all heaven, sing out;
clear the way for the coming of Cloud-Rider.
Enjoy God, cheer when you see him! Sing,
O kings of the earth!
Sing praises to the Lord! There he is: Sky-Rider,
striding the ancient skies.
Listen—he's calling in thunder, rumbling, rolling thunder.
Call out "Bravo!" to God, the High God of Israel.
His splendor and strength rise huge as thunderheads.
A terrible beauty, O God, streams from your sanctuary.
It's Israel's strong God!
He gives power and might to his people!
O you, his people—bless God!

Psalms 68: 1-4, 32-35

WHO AM I?

Today we are supposed to be having interesting weather patterns with storms and winds...& yet I listen now to the birds singing in joy of the day! People all over the internet and news are talking about the actions of two celebrities at a celebration event for them. I wonder what would happen if we as His people spent as much time in celebration of His glory and talking about His greatness and His actions? These verses say that His splendor and strength rise as thunderheads and as He strides across the heavens, the thunder echoes. What if we pictured the thunder as Him on the move? What if we truly pictured Him in His greatness and authority? What if we delighted in God's righteousness and sang/laughed in joy at His greatness when troubles came our way? What if we really truly saw God as the God He is? A God of power and might. A God above all kingdoms and authority. A God of wisdom and terrible beauty. Why terrible? Because that means tremendously above what I can imagine or think of...let's cheer God instead of the NFL! Let's put God first before anything in our lives. Let's celebrate Him first each day and have parties in His honor! Let's cheer Him at our ball games for making the day we play on. Let's begin to see things as they are through His eyes rather than our perception. Think of Him as the one who rides the clouds, commands the seas and walks the oceans. Think of Him as the wonderful creator He is! Delight in Him as you awaken. Refresh in Him as you sleep! Steep in Him throughout your day. He delights in you...maybe it's time you delighted yourself in Him...maybe it's time for you to take off the blinders and see Him for who He is. Nothing limits our God. Quit getting caught up in your circumstances and see Him. Way Maker, Miracle Worker, Promise Keeper, Light in the Darkness, Storm Speaker, Sky Rider, Cloud Walker, Peace Bringer,...who is He to you today?

Mortals make elaborate plans,
but God has the last word.
Humans are satisfied with whatever looks good;
God probes for what is good.
Put God in charge of your work,
then what you've planned will take place.
God made everything with a place and purpose;
even the wicked are included—but for judgment.
When God approves of your life,
even your enemies will end up shaking your hand.
We plan the way we want to live,
but only God makes us able to live it.

Proverbs 16: 1-4, 7, 9

MASTERPIECE!

Love this picture because you can see an overview of the grassland against the yellow river against the black beach against the ocean...it's like a terrific painting except it's natural the way God created it in the beginning. We look through things with mortal eyes and with an end of this life outlook and we miss the unseen. God has a plan and purpose for each thing/event/problem/celebration that occurs in our lives. He planned them just as He did the flow of this river and God allows us to make plans for our lives in accordance with His will. The issue is that sometimes we think well that looks/sounds like a good idea but God disagrees and puts things in our path to change our course much like a rock changes the course of a river. He has a directional tide to guide us and when you yield your desires to God, He will approve your life and bless you. This doesn't mean that there are not troubles that still come your way...a flowing river still has things that impede it and there are still times that God puts boulders in your way to redirect you through the course of life because He needs you to freshen and well up from the bottom of your heart so that you don't grow stagnant and putrid with your pride in yourself. God is constantly probing the thoughts and intents of your heart seeking His place and His desires for you. His plans for you are perfect but you must understand that His will should be accomplished and we are but tools in the Master's hands. I think of all the times I changed things around in my life to accommodate others and did so because it was in their best interest.

God is like this. He moves and lives and breathes to have communion with you. He created your innermost being and just like the butterfly poised to break out of that cocoon, He wants you to break out of the place of selfish pride and into His fullness so you can soar into His glory. He is for you. Let me say that again! He is FOR you. Better than a cheerleader at a game, God is the life coach who directs you on the field to the win but you must follow His directions and not get caught up in the moment. Press In. He's got amazing things for you. He desires to make you into the best of beautiful art in nature flowing in an elaborate pattern of grace so that all around can see and admire His handiwork and know that He is God. You are His masterpiece.

Trust God from the bottom of your heart;
don't try to figure out everything on your own.
Listen for God's voice in everything you do,
everywhere you go;
he's the one who will keep you on track.
Don't assume that you know it all.
Run to God! Run from evil!
Your body will glow with health,
your very bones will vibrate with life!
Honor God with everything you own;
give him the first and the best.
Your barns will burst,
your wine vats will brim over.
But don't, dear friend, resent God's discipline;
don't sulk under his loving correction.
It's the child he loves that God corrects;
a father's delight is behind all this.

Proverbs 3: 5-12

BOTTOMS UP!

Trust. Such a hard concept in our world that feels like quicksand. Listen. Hard in all the surround sound noise of our world. Run! Easy to do in fear and anguish, harder when the evil is so enticing. Honor. A lost concept in the world of me first. So how then is one to live a Christian life when all this is so hard?
Here's how:

Trust God and not your own eyes, beliefs or perceptions. Lean in. Press into Him through the hard. Listen for His voice guiding you through His word and your daily life by spending time soaking Him in for He is the anchor in the storm and the tracks that keep you aligned. You don't know or see all so trust that the God who created you does and press in. When it gets challenging, run to Him. Your whole being will vibrate with His presence and He will live/breathe through you. Give Him your very best not the tired, worn out part of you but the fresh and best part of you. Give it to Him in Honor each day as you spend time basking in Him. Don't resent the hard tests for these develop you into a Testimony. These corrections keep you on track, safe from harm, glowing vibrantly with His love. Tune out the voices around you and hear Him. You cannot do this without taking time to know His voice. You learn His voice by spending time in His word. His word is life. His word echoes through your day in everything you do. It's in the child's voice, the call of the bird, the buzz of the bees...it's beating in your heart and in your veins. His very being is in your core as He created you. A child from the womb knows His mother's voice because he heard it continuously for months. A child from the heart of God knows His voice because he hears it continuously too! I'm fascinated by the Northern Lights and would love to see them in person because they are an example of the tuning of magnetic frequencies in nature. God is playing a love song to mankind in these lights just as he does in the storms. His voice is there...but you must get still and quiet to hear Him. Stop the roar around you. Shut out the urgency of others. Get alone with the God of your heart and being. Bask in Him for He is calling to you.

Run from the noise.

Shut in with God.

Honor His presence with your full attention.

Listen to Him through His words.

Then TRUST.

Trust that No matter what He's got you.

That's true trust from the bottom of your heart.

We don't yet see things clearly. We're squinting in a fog, peering through a mist. But it won't be long before the weather clears and the sun shines bright! We'll see it all then, see it all as clearly as God sees us, knowing him directly just as he knows us! But for right now, until that completeness, we have three things to do to lead us toward that consummation: Trust steadily in God, hope unswervingly, love extravagantly. And the best of the three is love.

1 Corinthians 13: 12-13

THE FOG OF LIFE!

Until that completeness...for right now we have three jobs:

1. Trust steadily in God no matter the circumstances or the situation
2. Hope unswervingly without allowing doubt to steal our vision
3. Love extravagantly as God loves us without holding back in fear for ourselves.

When driving in the fog, it's very hard to see so you look carefully at the road markers and pacers set before you and you move steadily watching ahead and the relief you feel as the sun peeks through and clears the fog is refreshing.

For now, the road is foggy and we don't see the end. We must walk the path in front of us trusting God's unfailing hand that is guiding us with the roadmap of His word. We continue to place one foot in front of the other even as we walk in difficult places and valleys that are thick with fear/doubt because we cling to the hope that He is working things out and that the Son is coming. And throughout the journey we love with our whole being. Knowing that His love is why we are even here. His love is the road we are on. His love is the truth, the way and the light. His love is our guide. Trusting in His love is the only way to make it through the darkest nights when the fog is thick and steals your very breath. His love conquered death, hell, the grave once and for all. The harder one clings to the mile markers in this life, the more you miss the first rays of the Son as He appears. Jesus is coming soon and the evidence is all around. Get your eyes off yourself and your circumstances. Look into His Sonshine as it burns the fog of this life away from your vision so you can see His purpose. The mist is clearing...Jesus is working something beautiful even today!

Though the cherry trees don't blossom
and the strawberries don't ripen,
Though the apples are worm-eaten
and the wheat fields stunted,
Though the sheep pens are sheepless
and the cattle barns empty,
I'm singing joyful praise to God.
I'm turning cartwheels of joy to my
Savior God.
Counting on God's Rule to prevail,
I take heart and gain strength.
I run like a deer.
I feel like I'm king of the mountain!

Habakkuk 3:17-19

THE REPORT!

I woke to an audible voice at 2 AM this morning...it was the voice of God asking whose report will I believe. I know it was audible because my dogs started barking too. They heard and answered. You see nature responds to Him without thought. We try to explain it away in the natural, but it just is. God isn't a God caught up in our circumstances, He's a God of miracles. These verses in Habakkuk remind us that though times are hard and things look bleak, His ways are above our ways. It's time to get our heads and hearts out of the current circumstances and look beyond the lack to the One who created all. Sure the news reports that a food shortage is looming and gas prices are rising and money is getting tighter. Sure the doctors reports are that the cancer is deadly, the bones/muscles are weakening, the brain isn't all it should be...sure the wars rage, the tornadoes rip, the rain/lightning rage around us but these are all the surroundings, the background. Yesterday I went with my staff to a very impressive immersive experience of art through sound, color, lights and it was all encompassing...I thought as my senses exploded with all the lights and sounds how overwhelming and explosive that moment surrounding me was...what if I took in God like this?

What if I let His light, joy, words, emotions explode through me in this vast way? Sure, the circumstances can look dire and the reports can be negative BUT GOD...BUT GOD...BUT GOD...GOD is the same God who told the Red Sea to stand aside and let the Israelites walk through. He's still the God who chose a young girl to become a queen to save His people. He's still the same God who healed lepers and changed water to wine. He's still the same God who caused the blind to see, the deaf to hear, the lame to walk. Cancer doesn't scare Him. Circumstances cannot dictate Him. There is nothing bigger than our God. Get out of your own head. Quit looking at the waves around you. Reach up to His unchanging hand. He's still God. What if He chooses to move in another way than you think He should? He's GOD! Let Him reign over you. Let Him calm you, hold you, speak to you and LISTEN! The circumstances don't look good...so what? Start singing, start praising, let His joy fill you despite your circumstances.

Take heart, gain strength! Run to Him with all your heart! He's GOD! He's called you His own! Embrace Him through the trials and circumstances. Hold Him close! Feel like the king's child because you are! Whose report will you believe? I choose JOY! I choose God's RULE. His rule says we are His! The sheep of His pasture! The blossoms on His trees. The fruit of His labor! I choose to BELIEVE! Y'all it's getting exciting up in here! My neighbors may think I'm crazy but I choose to believe! Let the burdens go. Bask in His goodness! You are not of this world so quit letting it define your circumstances! He is GOD not a god...THE GOD of all the universe and He cares for you. Are you catching it now? Yes, things may look bad around you BUT GOD! Rise up! Bring a Hallelujah to your circumstances! Shout to The Lord! Truly He is worthy and His joy is what I have! The world didn't give it and the world cannot take it away!! It's all because of Jesus! King of my heart! Whose report are you listening to? The report of the circumstances or the report of the Creator?

"Give your entire attention to what God is doing right now, and don't get worked up about what may or may not happen tomorrow. God will help you deal with whatever hard things come up when the time comes.
Matthew 6:34

ATTENTION!

Confession time: I am always having to put this verse in my heart as I am a fretter...my mom used to sing to me. ♪ Why worry when you can pray, trust Jesus, He'll be your stay. Don't be a doubting Thomas, lean fully on His promises. Why worry, worry, worry, worry...when you can pray! ♪ she's right you know.

Sunday night in the middle of the night I had a small fall and hurt my back so that I could barely walk on Monday. Then on Tuesday I couldn't walk at all. On Wednesday I went to go see the doctor and got x-rays and a steroid shot and a scheduled MRI. Naturally the worry started but then I remembered his promises and I remembered that even though there is pain, his promises are stronger. I began to give my entire attention to what God was doing instead of what my body was doing and before you know it the pain had begun to alleviate and my spirit was encouraged and uplifted. We got some bad news in several situations including my uncle Robert having a major health issue that needs lots of prayer and a miracle. The truth is, it is really easy to get discouraged, but when our focus is on Him and not on us, it changes things. This doesn't mean that we don't do what the doctors tell us to do because yes I got a shot yesterday and an x-ray and I did my PT and I will continue to do the things to take care of this physical body.

But I also realize that this is just a temporary home for my spirit. I must realize that God is doing dynamic things and his purpose will be worked up on this earth with me or without me. So I must choose to be a part of that and if I do remember not to get worked up and to continue in his way taking one step at a time, one day at a time trusting in his promises then I get his complete peace that passes all understanding. You see this promise is one that we can truly cling to because it says if we pay attention to him and what he is doing then he will walk with us each step of the way taking one step at a time and he will make our way straight. A few days ago there was some tornadoes and High winds and I watched at my house as there was one little plant clinging to a rock some mossy like stuff and the wind ripped at it and ripped at it and ripped at it and yet it never moved and I was fascinated by that...that this hard wind ripping at this little piece of Moss and it never moved. You see it was rooted deeply into the rock. I needed that. We who are rooted in Him need to be like that moss, for although the winds of life may tear at us, we stay rooted in His promises knowing that He is able and He WILL work for us on our behalf in all situations. Today and each day I will be walking in constant prayer for miracles. I believe that God is about to reveal himself in a super powerful way to this world and it's going to be through me and you because we are His hands extended! Who needs a miracle? We all do and He is the God of miracles. Thank you God for being our source. Press in Folks. Miracles are coming. Give your ENTIRE attention to Him and not your situation. He's got you!

Summing up: Be agreeable, be sympathetic, be loving, be compassionate, be humble. That goes for all of you, no exceptions. No retaliation. No sharp-tongued sarcasm. Instead, bless— that's your job, to bless.
You'll be a blessing and also get a blessing.
Whoever wants to embrace life
and see the day fill up with good,
Here's what you do:
Say nothing evil or hurtful;
Snub evil and cultivate good;
run after peace for all you're worth.
God looks on all this with approval,
listening and responding well to what he's asked;
But he turns his back
on those who do evil things.

1 Peter 3: 8-12

SUM IT UP!

This scripture screams the TRUTH! My favorite part is that God looks at what you do in your day to day and approves those things that are uplifting. When you cultivate peace and embrace life's goodness, He looks on you and meets your needs, wants and desires. Sometimes things don't go as you'd like and you feel the weight of the world on you but then...He steps up and takes charge. I'll admit that today has been a hard day for me as have the last few because my heart is hurting for my family members who are struggling with hard things and my physical body has suffered yet another setback but then His blessings come like a wave of encouragement lifting me up above the shadows. These blessings come in His word and through others. They come in my memories and in my every day. I choose to count them on the hard days. This verse is perfect! Sum it up...it means to make it short and sweet but also it means to add. If I add all my blessings up and choose to be agreeable, sympathetic, loving, compassionate, humble, and cultivate good by pursuing peace...then God looks on me and smiles with that "favorite child" smile. I don't have to be perfect. I just have to choose well, embrace life and be a blessing to those around me in my best way possible. This is what fills my day with good. If you're having a bad day, count it all JOY. Count the good and the good will fill up. Count the bad and it will overwhelm. Choose. Add up the good and I promise it will turn your day around. Lord, I thank you that on my bad days, you have given me a way to escape them through your promises. I thank you that you have given me the tools to choose good and to pursue peace. I ask that you give me your grace and mercy daily so I might do the same by filling others up with your blessings. I ask for a special sense of peace for my aunt Bonnie and a miraculous healing for my uncle Robert. I ask for your move in my body and strength to face any circumstances ahead in our lives. I thank you for all you do.

PS: please answer the small need and the big because they are equal in the lives of many...Because of who you are I give you glory, even if things don't go my way! And I thank you in advance for knowing my every need before I even ask.

For thus says the Lord: After seventy years are completed at Babylon, I will visit you and perform My good word toward you, and cause you to return to this place. For I know the thoughts that I think toward you, says the Lord, thoughts of peace and not of evil, to give you a future and a hope. Then you will call upon Me and go and pray to Me, and I will listen to you. And you will seek Me and find Me, when you search for Me with all your heart. I will be found by you, says the Lord, and I will bring you back from your captivity; I will gather you from all the nations and from all the places where I have driven you, says the Lord, and I will bring you to the place from which I cause you to be carried away captive.

Jereimah 29: 10-14

CONTEXT CLUES!

Context matters in any situation but especially in God's word. The context for Jeremiah 29:11 that so many like to quote is important because it shows us a God who has delved out discipline to his people. That particular verse is a promise with a contingency...after the discipline, He will come perform the good word. Then the people will call on God, pray and He will listen. Seeking God and finding Him involves following after His heart. We live in a very fickle world who thinks that God follows them and even falsely attributes their works & deeds to God when He isn't in it. You will not find God's hand in the building of a casino or place of ill repute and yet people try to put him there with their "thanking God" or prayers and blessings over these places. This will become more and more rampant. This past week I saw a "church" at a "dedication" service for a family planning clinic that included abortions for certain situations. God was not in that. Elijah sought God and a storm came as he looked but God wasn't in the storm. God was in a still small voice in his consciousness. This picture of a storm behind the scripture is quite overwhelming and mighty looking but God isn't in the storm...He calms the storms. I'm not saying He doesn't allow them or use them. I'm saying that God isn't in everything that man attributes to Him and is in many things not attributed to Him. Discipline is a small thing that makes a big difference. You must be disciplined to get into God's word and truly seek Him. Do not only rely on others to feed you but dive into His word so that you can divine for yourself His purposes in your life and grow in Him. God's after you. He will chase you down to capture your heart as He loves you with an everlasting love. But do not think that there is not discipline for the running. He chastises us because He cares for us. Why did God wait 70 years to complete His word in the people of Israel in this situation? He wanted a generation of rebellion to die off. He wanted a people eager for release from their situation of captivity. He wanted people who would see Him for who He is. It is important we examine this because America has become a wayward nation just as Israel was...America has thumbed its nose at God and this disdain doesn't come without discipline. Any good parenting requires discipline in a wayward and rebellious youth...but know after the discipline comes the renewal. It's time to seek God with all our hearts so that this time of rebellion can be quelled and God's purpose can reign once again. He will be found in that still small voice when you pray and seek Him with all your heart.

God is a safe place to hide,
ready to help when we need him.
We stand fearless at the cliff-edge of doom,
courageous in seastorm and earthquake,
Before the rush and roar of oceans,
the tremors that shift mountains.
Jacob-wrestling God fights for us,
God-of-Angel-Armies protects us. Attention, all!
See the marvels of God!
He plants flowers and trees all over the earth,
Bans war from pole to pole,
breaks all the weapons across his knee.
"Step out of the traffic! Take a long,
loving look at me, your High God,
above politics, above everything."

Psalms 46: 1-3, 8-10

A SAFE PLACE!

Jacob wrestling God, God of Angel Armies, marvelous God, God of the safe place, God of refuge, High God above politics and all else...these are the descriptions of God that David used in this small selection of verses...I have often read over those without listening to them but there is a message in each name...

If you are needing a place of refuge from the storms of war or life...He is ready to help whenever you NEED Him, not just when you call out. Makes me think of a child whose parent sees and knows that they are close to the edge and just as they begin to tumble, the parent grabs them before they even realize they need to cry out. Having confidence in this allows you to stand fearless on the cliff edge, courageous in the storms of life from the earthquakes of illness to the sea storms of financial strain to the edge of life itself no matter what roars and shakes you.

The Jacob wrestling God is the one who gets down and dirty with you fighting for your very soul against the gates of hell. He's the one who reigns as your conscience telling you to listen and hear. He's the one who despite your willfulness continues to work on your behalf even though you haven't recognized Him as King of all. He's willing to fight you for you and sometimes that's a painful wrestling that you may not understand as Jacob did not and it isn't without scars as Jacob retained a limp from God touching his hip in this wrestling. It's a place of God taking you to who He wants you to be.
God of Angel Armies is the God of Peace and War. He creates all beauty and habitat from flowers and bees to birds and trees...the moon and the stars themselves recognize & obey His very words and yet...He commands armies of angels who protect and war on our behalf from pole to pole...He's in control.

He is The High God. Not one of a series but the Only above all other gods who would make themselves such through political gain and power. He is above everything! There is no cancer that can hide from Him, there is no Ruler who can overcome Him, there is no kingdom that can outlast Him, there is no weapon that can overpower him. He's greater than a superhero. He's bigger than our imagination and stronger than any government. There is nothing our God cannot do! And yet...

He desires a relationship with you. Step out of your busyness of day to day traffic and look lovingly at all your God has done and begin to see what He will do. Quit becoming overwhelmed with your day to day struggle against the seemingly impossible circumstances and SEE Him. LISTEN to Him. His love for you is everlasting. He is the God of all and yet He desires a moment with you. He's not a puppy to patiently wait for your attention and He's not a genie who is waiting to perform your commands. He is GOD! He will find you, wrestle with you..for He desires good things for you and you are His.

Taste and See that God is Good!

But whoever catches a glimpse of the revealed counsel of God—the free life!—even out of the corner of his eye, and sticks with it, is no distracted scatterbrain but a man or woman of action. That person will find delight and affirmation in the action.

James 1: 25

GET YOUR GLASSES ON!

A woman of action that is filled with delight and affirmation…what a description…who, you might ask? Me, you, anyone who catches a glimpse of God's purpose and is all about it…not about self but about Him. It is so easy to get distracted in our everyday struggle by the things around us and to lose the focus of eternity. Sometimes we just take off the "vision of God" like a pair of glasses we removed and get caught up in the natural. The natural says things are not possible. God says I'm the God of the impossible. The natural says things are bad, God says I make all things good in my time. Natural dictates fear of the future and things to come but God says I make all things new and I didn't give you a spirit of fear but of love and a sound mind. Catch a glimpse today…open His word…surround yourself with His promises. He says it , I believe and that settles it. Recently I heard someone say that God isn't enough…boy did they lose focus…God's word says He is ALL…the beginning and the end, the everlasting and the eternity. You see part of this is not just catching the glimpse of God but sticking with it when the glimpse keeps trying to fade. Have you caught a glimpse of His promises but it keeps trying to slip away in the cares of the day? Refocus. Put your "God's vision" glasses back on. It's time to look beyond your circumstances and your limitations to what He will do through you if you'll let Him. Today, Lord, I aim to catch a glimpse of you through the revealing counsel of your word and to stick with it no matter the distractions so I can be deemed a woman of God, filled with delightful actions that show your love and mercy! Give me your wisdom, strength and faith so I may keep focused in this battle of the mind.

Consider it a sheer gift, friends, when tests and challenges come at you from all sides. You know that under pressure, your faith-life is forced into the open and shows its true colors. So don't try to get out of anything prematurely. Let it do its work so you become mature and well-developed, not deficient in any way. Anyone who meets a testing challenge head-on and manages to stick it out is mighty fortunate. For such persons loyally in love with God, the reward is life and more life.

James 1: 2-4, 12

SHEER GIFTS!

What a privilege it is to walk the faith life!! Today's challenges come to you to develop you into a mature fighter in the spiritual battle which is in play. When pressure comes, it makes you press in. When tests & challenges come, they hone your skills by making you PRESS into Him. Consider it a gift. Let it do the work that God intends it to do. Everyone experiences challenges and tests...but not all have the tools and skills to excel at these. The tools and skills come from the pressing into His Spirit and walking closely in relationship. A warrior battling gets tired and sometimes beat up by the battle but those that are honed through these fires become better at the spiritual warfare and less likely to fade and fall. We are in a spiritual war for the souls of mankind. If we begin to get bogged down by the fray around us, then our adversary roars in celebration not realizing that through our trials we can become stronger on the battleground. I think of the Christians in Ukraine right now who are feeling the physical war as well as the spiritual war...this is a battle of pure evil. We walk in light. His LIGHT-His SONLIGHT! Let us not be misled by the fray or propaganda of the enemy. When our minds turn to earthly solutions to spiritual battles, we are caught and must battle our way out in the Spirit. Yes, it seems everywhere you turn today, Christians are in the battle but that is as it should be. Don't think for one minute that it is not our purpose. Our purpose is not to be here for our pleasure nor to walk in ease. Our purpose is to battle the evil and all that our adversary who seeks to destroy throws at us. Our battlefield is the mind, heart and souls of men/women/children. Our battlefield is not of our making although we do create some of our own battles without purpose. Without a TEST you cannot have a TESTimony! Consider this gift. For from this gift you are being honed and rewarded with a stronger faith and LIFE! The LIFE that no other can give. Remember the battlefield and don't be distracted by the journey around you. Focus on Him and His purpose within you. You may feel like your colors are purple and blue with bruises from the battle but this forces your faith life into the open so the battle colors of Jesus' blood washing away every stain and leaving you white as snow and pure can shine. Wars leave scars and wars damage but the Life everlasting is worth the battle! Consider the SHEER gift...for now we see through a glass darkly but soon we shall see Face to Faith!

You who sit down in the High God's presence,
spend the night in Shaddai's shadow,
Say this: "God, you're my refuge.
I trust in you and I'm safe!"
That's right—he rescues you from hidden traps,
shields you from deadly hazards.
His huge outstretched arms protect you—
under them you're perfectly safe;
his arms fend off all harm.
Fear nothing—not wild wolves in the night,
not flying arrows in the day,
Not disease that prowls through the darkness,
not disaster that erupts at high noon.
Even though others succumb all around,
drop like flies right and left,
no harm will even graze you.
You'll stand untouched, watch it all from a distance,
watch the wicked turn into corpses.
Yes, because God's your refuge,
the High God your very own home,
Evil can't get close to you,
harm can't get through the door.
He ordered his angels
to guard you wherever you go.
If you stumble, they'll catch you;
their job is to keep you from falling.
You'll walk unharmed among lions and snakes,
and kick young lions and serpents from the path.

Psalms 91: 1-13

IN THE SHADOW!

Recently I had a conversation with someone who expressed frustration with these promises of God because his life has not been easy and he has had a lot of disappointments, frustrations and downright evil in his life. The question was if God is so true to His promises then why do so many good Godly people have sicknesses, problems and death. Why must I suffer if God's promises here are true? The truth is that it is easy to focus on the earthly problems, situations and issues as they consume us day to day but let's examine this from a different point of view. You...who sit down in the High God's presence...now who is this You? It's the ethereal you...the spiritual being...the soul of your essence. That's right. You. See if You are dwelling in His presence then the things of this world are not nearly as weighty. Yes, He protects this earthly being that houses the soul and many times we experience that mercy and recognize it as an heavenly intervention. The thing is we often get caught up in this "earthly" as being the place of the promises delivered much like the Children of Israel in the wilderness. Yes God guided and protected them there but 'there" they also had many trials because it was not the Promised Land. The focus or perspective matters. If your focus is eternal then the happening on Earth does not have the same weight. Yes, God is concerned in your everyday life because He is your Father and loves you but His focus is on your eternity not just your immediate. He says Fear Nothing because He is your HOME. Home is a place of safety, peace, trust, relaxation. If God is truly your home then the things of this world cannot consume you. Sure they matter as they are a part of your journey but if you shift perspective, you can enjoy even the bumps and lumps. You can see them for what they are...a place of growing and learning, a place of spiritual battle and a place of ultimate victory for God prepared you a way of escape from even the slightest of temptations. Isn't it time you shifted your focus? Get your eyes off the things keeping you from seeing His perspective. Shift your view by diving into His promises. Spend the night in His shadow, His covering. Relax and let God. That problem that looks insurmountable...does it matter in eternity? Will it change where you spend eternity or affect how another spends eternity? Perspective...a small thing that sure makes a big difference. My God, my refuge, please allow me to shift my perspective heavenward. Help me to look upon my circumstances with your eyes, your perspective, a view through the eyes of eternity. Help me to get my eyes off the here and now so I may focus on your purpose in my life.

Open your mouth and taste,
open your eyes and see—how good God is.
Blessed are you who run to him.
Worship God if you want the best;
worship opens doors to all his goodness.
Is anyone crying for help?
God is listening, ready to rescue you.
If your heart is broken, you'll find God right there;
if you're kicked in the gut,
he'll help you catch your breath.
He's your bodyguard, shielding every bone;
not even a finger gets broken.

Psalms 34: 8-9, 17-18, 20

WORSHIP IS THE KEY!

I think this Stone's getting ready to roll - I feel a faith that is starting to rise

And I see a world on the edge of revival - I think it's only a matter of time

So, do what only you can do - Move what only you can move

Even the impossible is possible for you - I see a grave that is hollow of power

I see a battle that's already won - And I see a church on the verge of revival

I see your kingdom has already come - So, do what only you can do

Move what only you can move - Even the impossible is possible for you

You can make the chains come loose - You can tell the mountains move

Even the impossible is possible for you - Even the impossible is possible for you

You said it, I see it - You still do miracles

There's power in Jesus name - All darkness defeated

There's nothing stopping you, my God - There's nothing stopping you

You said it, I see it - You still do miracles

There's power in Jesus name - All darkness defeated

There's nothing stopping you, my God - There's nothing stopping you

Do what only you can do - Move what only you can move

Even the impossible is possible for you - You can make the chains come loose

You can tell the mountains move - Even the impossible is possible for you

Even the impossible is possible for you - You said it, I see it

You still do miracles - There's power in Jesus name

All darkness defeated - There's nothing stopping you, my God

There's nothing stopping you - You said it, I see it

You still do miracles - There's power in Jesus name

All darkness defeated

There's nothing stopping you, my God

There's nothing stopping you

There's nothing stopping you

O Lord, You have searched me and known me.
You know my sitting down and my rising up;
You understand my thought afar off.
You comprehend my path and my lying down,
And are acquainted with all my ways.

Search me, O God, and know my heart;
Try me, and know my anxieties;
And see if there is any wicked way in me,
And lead me in the way everlasting.

Psalms 139: 1-3, 23-24

SEARCH AND DIRECT!

I love this song of David's as he begins with the knowing that God is omniscient and knows him intimately. He continues through recognition that God created each of us in the womb and knew us before we knew ourselves. He understands our situations from the beginning of time. The intimacy of this recognition is then taken from you know me to please know me in all my ways because David recognizes that God allows us free will. Yes, He knows you and exactly what is going on with you. He has plans for you from the beginning of time but He also gives you free will. I think of all the times I planned in advance wonderful things for my kids and then because of their choices, the plans were skewed or changed or had less than what I had purposed for them. I didn't quit loving them or become angry with them. I redirected them in a loving manner, cleaned up their messes and although my heart hurt for the things/experiences lost, I picked up and went on with my thoughts and plans for their future. God sees much more than we do. His plans are much higher. When our hands are in it and we feel like failures, He's still there waiting with open arms. Life is a journey with many adventures. He's the creator of all and knows what lies ahead. I think it's time to just trust His plans and walk in His ways. Like David, my prayer is Search me, O God. Find any wicked way in me and cleanse me. Direct me in your ways so I may be used by you.

King David went in, took his place before God, and prayed: "Who am I, my Master God, and what is my family, that you have brought me to this place in life? But that's nothing compared to what's coming, for you've also spoken of my family far into the future, given me a glimpse into tomorrow, my Master God! What can I possibly say in the face of all this? You know me, Master God, just as I am. You've done all this not because of who I am but because of who you are—out of your very heart!—but you've let me in on it. "This is what makes you so great, Master God! There is none like you, no God but you, nothing to compare with what we've heard with our own ears. And who is like your people, like Israel, a nation unique in the earth, whom God set out to redeem for himself (and became most famous for it), performing great and fearsome acts, throwing out nations and their gods left and right as you saved your people from Egypt? You established for yourself a people—your very own Israel!—your people permanently. And you, God, became their God.

2 Samuel 7: 18-24

FIRE ME UP!

♫ "God, You are great, you do miracles so great...there is no one else like you, there is no else like you" ♪ "Not because of what I've done but because of who you are...I am a flower quickly fading...here today and gone tomorrow, a-wave in the ocean, a whisper in the wind, still you hear me when I'm calling and catch me when I'm falling, remind me who I am...for I am yours" ♫

God's promises are good for you and true and redemptive. God's promises are for always. Who are we to Him? We are His. It is in recognition of this place that He uses us as His hands extended. He knows you just as you are and He wants you to know Him more intimately just as He is and just because of who He is.

David is called a man after God's heart because He craved God's attention and yearned for Him. He sought Him and he found Him for His word says if we seek Him, we will find Him. David was given a great legacy in that Jesus was born into his lineage because God chose Mary who was yielded. David's legacy was one of riches and fame but also heartache and doubt. He had tragedy and triumph. He had extreme lows and desperation and he had celebration and power. When asked which he preferred, He said he'd rather be a doorkeeper in the house of God...than to dwell in the richness of evil. Think on this. No matter what your situation today, you have the choice to become a doorkeeper...better yet, just like the Prodigal son, Jesus welcomes you with open arms and has a table spread in your honor with a feast. Come. It's time.

Lord, I am amazed by you constantly. I tell you my needs and I trust in your provision. I come to you with my heart knowing you are the beat that makes it work. I come to you with my mind knowing you are the creator of every synapse that fires. Renew my spirit in you. Refresh me with your living water. Make me like you.

My dear children, you come from God and belong to God. You have already won a big victory over those false teachers, for the Spirit in you is far stronger than anything in the world. These people belong to the Christ-denying world. They talk the world's language and the world eats it up. But we come from God and belong to God. Anyone who knows God understands us and listens. The person who has nothing to do with God will, of course, not listen to us. This is another test for telling the Spirit of Truth from the spirit of deception.

1 John 4: 4-6

LISTEN TO UNDERSTAND!

Understanding is a skill derived from another skill...it requires listening which requires hearing which requires attention which requires focus which requires intention. I recently read comments on a thread of a post from The White House and it was interesting to see those completely deceived and those who have clarity in the way the comments spiraled. Yes, I read comments for fun...it is really comical sometimes that people sit behind a phone or computer and truly say things I bet they would never say in person.

This picture is of an oil rig in the ocean that supplies a necessary product to our lives. Many of us have never seen one in our lives yet we rely on it being there. Many people live on this rig for weeks/months at a time to supply our needs and those of their families and it is a hard life. It is a dwelling place for those who live/work there but it is temporary and not their real home. They know this even though it has the things they need to live and it provides resources. What is my point? This world is not our home. It is just a temporary shelter of resources but it is not the place we should root.

Victory In our lives over falsenesses comes from dwelling in the plane of The Spirit and not in the falsehood of the flesh. Understanding is a gift of the Spirit. It comes from dwelling in the place of spiritual knowledge and not allowing the falseness to take root.

Intention...the root of understanding. Getting to the purpose behind a message whether it is commentary or statement requires seeing the intention. Seeing the intentions requires spiritual knowledge and wisdom that comes from the Source.

John is writing to instruct us that there is a spiritual plane and that The Spirit of God which dwells in us gives us the gift to read through the words into the intention of the heart...seeing the purpose behind the comments.
The spirit of deception is rampant in our world from every source. The Spirit of Truth however is much more powerful and cannot be deceived If we walk in The Light, the lies and deceptions cannot hide the truth because He dwells in us.
So...here's the test. Does what is being said line up with His word and His Spirit within you?

A deceptive word, comment or deed doesn't align with God's Spirit and no matter how one tries, cannot hide from God's truth. Telling the truth from deception is that simple. Look into the intentions. The Spirit of God dwelling in you is stronger than any lies the deceived try to put out. But the key is in the dwelling. If you dwell in His Spirit then the deceptions are immediately obvious and stand out as such.

Anyone can hide things but only The Spirit can reveal the Truth behind any deception.

Don't fret or worry. Instead of worrying, pray. Let petitions and praises shape your worries into prayers, letting God know your concerns. Before you know it, a sense of God's wholeness, everything coming together for good, will come and settle you down. It's wonderful what happens when Christ displaces worry at the center of your life.

Philippians 4: 6-7

NO FRETTING ALLOWED?

🎼 Jesus at the center of it all! Jesus at the center of it all. From beginning to the end, it will always be it's always been you Jesus, Jesus...nothing else matters, nothing in this world will do. Jesus at the center, everything revolves around you Jesus...Jesus...Jesus at the center of my life... 🎵

Hoping your heart is singing that song now. Worry displaces God's peace but praise displaces worry and recenters your life. Where you put your focus matters! Last month was a really rough and tough month for me and occasionally I let worry tilt my focus which disrupted my sense of wholeness and peace. But, He was still always there like the moon He put into the sky. The moon is always there, only we don't focus on it or see it many times because we aren't looking for it. God is the same yesterday, today and forever. When we get off kilter and begin to focus on the mess that man has made from high gas prices to war to our own cosmos of difficulties...we are centered on us and the problems which tilts our attention away from Him and into chaos and darkness, but through praise, we can recenter on Him and find our joy. Walk outside. The moon is in the sky. Move around until you are only seeing one thing and focus. What happened? You zoned in on it. You looked diligently and you found it.

Your mind centered on finding it. Imagine now...God...the center of the universe...the creator of all mankind. Focus on Him. Center on Him. Let the worries go as you seek Him only. Feel His praise in your heart, mind, being...let Him fill you. Jesus at the center of it all...Lord, I am so very grateful for your love and mercy that are new every morning. Great is your faithfulness. As I recenter my life, thoughts and plans on you...bring peace to me. Be my everything today and let me be a beacon of light to another as the moon reflects the light of the sun...let me reflect the light of your Son. Jesus at the center of my life... always.

"Don't bargain with God. Be direct. Ask for what you need. This is not a cat-and-mouse, hide-and-seek game we're in. If your little boy asks for a serving of fish, do you scare him with a live snake on his plate? If your little girl asks for an egg, do you trick her with a spider? As bad as you are, you wouldn't think of such a thing—you're at least decent to your own children. And don't you think the Father who conceived you in love will give the Holy Spirit when you ask him?"

Luke 11: 10-13

THE BARGAIN!

Bargaining is done when one is unsure of the value, the fixed price or cost of something. Bargaining is done when one feels like they are in competition or uncertain of the acceptance. Luke is writing as an advisor here that God isn't cheap. He's not someone who will fleece you or trick you. God isn't unsure of you or your value. Luke compares our requests to God as the request of a child for necessary food. The Spiritual realm is very real and God has wonderful gifts of healing, miracles, faith, spiritual languages and interpretations as well as many other gifts. He desires to give these gifts to us so we might operate in a higher plane than just this earthly one. It's not a trick nor even hard but a simple asking. I was 11 when I asked God to fill me with His Holy Spirit. I had never asked before with a desire to grow closer to Him. I was determined that night that I would wait on Him to reveal His gift to me and He did. Over the years, He has used me in various ways through gifts of languages and interpretations, visions, healings, etc. but these gifts aren't mine...they are God's and He pours them into a person who is yielded. Why does He fill some and not others in a "timely" manner? God knows us. He sees our innermost thoughts and understands us at a different level. I remember being a little irritated when I was growing up because God used certain people in gifts that I thought weren't worthy. He chastised me that He will use the yielded vessels as He sees fit. The Holy Spirit is the comforter who walks with you and draws you closer to Him. Ask Him. Ask Him today to draw closer. His gifts are priceless. Be direct. He knows you better than you know yourself. God sees your value even if you don't. Lord, I thank you that you created me in my innermost being and you know me better than I know myself. Often I am filled with self doubt but through you, I feel loved & valued. Today I humbly ask for you to fill me to overflowing with your amazing spirit and the gifts of your heavenly languages so that our communication is on another plane. I ask you to touch lives around me like a spark jumping around igniting the flames. Thank you for being who you are. Because of who you are, I give you glory. Not only because of what you've done but because you are my everything! I love you Lord!

My dear children, let's not just talk about love; let's practice real love. This is the only way we'll know we're living truly, living in God's reality. It's also the way to shut down debilitating self-criticism, even when there is something to it. For God is greater than our worried hearts and knows more about us than we do ourselves.

1 John 3: 18-20

THE PRACTICE!

A couple of days ago I was headed home late from work and decided to swing through and grab fast food as I hadn't had time to eat. There was a long line so I waited a long time and the hunger pains were real by the time I got my food. As I was pulling out, thinking I was only seconds away from grabbing a bite, a woman stepped right in front of my car and I rolled down the window to tell her how dangerous it was. God spoke to my heart and told me to give her my sack of food. I actually argued with Him because I was hungry! I said I'll give her part and He said No, give it all. My rebellious spirit (yes I'm a little stubborn) argued again...(God, I waited a long time, I haven't eaten today...and it's still a good distance home...) again, He prompted...ALL! So I rolled the window back down and ungraciously held the sack out the window...about that time I heard a mewling sound and saw a small baby hand come from her coat. On this cold, rainy night...this mom was out trying to get food for her kid. I couldn't stand it. I stopped the car, got out in the rain and then proceeded to do what needed to be done for the least of these. This mom had been thrown out by her abusive boyfriend and was doing all she could. I changed my plans and took her to a place of safety for battered women. My hunger faded as my spirit was filled with His presence. I had no intention of sharing this with anyone as this was a moment that God showed me the truth behind the lights. People are hurting everywhere and we have the ability to be the light if we could see beyond ourselves. I thank God that He showed me and gave me this opportunity.

It's inconvenient and uncomfortable but it's why He calls us to be His hands extended. Practicing love takes us out of ourselves and our worries about our own situation. Whose reality will you see today? God, I ask you to open my eyes to the hurting and give me means to be your hands, your heart, your spirit to the hurting world around me.

Who can find a virtuous wife?
For her worth is far above rubies.
The heart of her husband safely trusts her;
So he will have no lack of gain.
She does him good and not evil
All the days of her life.
Strength and honor are her clothing;
She shall rejoice in time to come.
She opens her mouth with wisdom,
And on her tongue is the law of kindness.
Her children rise up and call her blessed;
Her husband also, and he praises her:
Charm is deceitful and beauty is passing,
But a woman who fears the Lord, she shall be praised.
Give her of the fruit of her hands,
And let her own works praise her in the gates.

Proverbs 31: 10-12, 25-26, 28, 30-31

THE WOMAN OF GREAT VALUE!

Today is International Women's Day but God says every day is a Proverbs 31 Woman's Day.

A woman after God's heart is described through the wisdom of Solomon in Proverbs 31. It is a blueprint for a woman blessed of God. Lots of people get into debates of the role of women in the workplace, the home, the church, etc. but the truth is that it was a woman who changed our world in the beginning by a poor choice of seeking outside the bounds of God's design and it was a woman who yielded her body to His purpose and brought the light of God back to Earth through the birth of the Savior. God created woman with a special purpose and design. He has a special heart place for women and desires all of us to be fulfilled in His purpose. As a woman, there are so many times we can see in scripture that women were instrumental in God's plans but every time, it required a yielding. Each time of yielding initiated a time of deliverance. Esther yielded her fear for such a time as she was called and became a ruler of historic proportions. Ruth yielded her home & all she knew to follow her mother in law which led her to great love and being a part of the lineage of Christ. Rahab yielded her safety for spies and was saved along with her family...Anna yielded her own plans and was allowed to hold Christ incarnate. A yielded woman is the most powerful force on Earth as she touches the heart of God. A woman yielded, broken and spilled out sees the anointing of God. Today I pray for all the women in my life. I pray for their yielding of themselves to His purpose. Lord, take me, a woman designed for your purpose. Mold me into a vessel and offering so that I may be used by you. A vessel of honor oh God...a vessel that is sanctified and holy...make me a vessel of honor for you.

Every God-born person conquers the world's ways. The conquering power that brings the world to its knees is our faith. The person who wins out over the world's ways is simply the one who believes Jesus is the Son of God. My purpose in writing is simply this: that you who believe in God's Son will know beyond the shadow of a doubt that you have eternal life, the reality and not the illusion. And how bold and free we then become in his presence, freely asking according to his will, sure that he's listening. And if we're confident that he's listening, we know that what we've asked for is as good as ours.

1 John 5: 4-5, 13-15

PROTUBERANCE!

Yesterday morning I looked out the window and I saw a flower on a rose bush that didn't look like the others. It got my attention and stood out so much I had to go see it, smell it, take it to be a special flower but in doing so I also cut it away from that which gave it life. I brought it in and put it in water with other flowers but its uniqueness still struck me as it was one among many but still outstanding! Then my dad sent me a word (protuberant) which I knew in a whole different context...but he sent it with scripture which I would never have connected with. My mind pondered it.

Last evening, I worked with a couple of kiddos who in their uniqueness were non compliant so needed my special attention. They needed to be heard and allowed their moment of fight to be felt and understood by another. I spoke with several men/women of God yesterday who have that innate quality of standing out in their lives and drawing a lot of ire for their stance. Then as I ran an errand I heard a pastor say on the radio that authority isn't earned but rather given only by God. It is a mantle that rests upon you and makes you stand out.

You see, over and over God was speaking His word to me yesterday if I tuned in, but this morning it came together as I read that we as God's people stand out by conquering the world's ways and walking in FAITH! What makes you an outstanding person who is protuberant and walking in authority of Jesus Christ is the Faith that moves mountains. You embrace the reality over the illusion. When I was young, I read a book called The Emperor's Clothes. The Emperor was always wanting to be the one who stood out so he was constantly pushing the boundaries with his clothes. The people of his kingdom tolerated his nonsense and bowed to his ways so much that when a tailor told the emperor, in fear of not making the perfect garment, that he had on invisible clothes, the people all around acquiesced to it and admired his "clothes". As he marched through the town, everyone admired his new "invisible clothes" until a child who stood out in clarity not bound by deception shouted out...he's naked! How bold and free that child was because he had not bought into the illusion but rather saw the reality and walked freely in it. The church of God, the bride of Christ has fallen for the illusion of the world called "science" and embraced the nakedness of this into our lives. Understand that I am not against science until it stands completely at odds with God's word just like I am not against clothes but I can tell when one is naked even if "science" says it's invisible clothes. This isn't a political post...It's a God post. We have walked too long in the ways of the world that we have traded the faith that makes us swell with God's presence and stand out in protuberance for a false reality and illusion. We have walked in the fear of the false mantle for so long that we have forgotten whose authority was given. We are walking by a worldly sight rather than by faith. When we walk by faith, we walk in confidence knowing that what we ask-in Jesus' name, it is done. When we put on the mantle of authority in His name, all power is given so that we can command a sickness to leave, a place in our bodies to be healed and have complete confidence in Him that it will be done according to His purpose. I have walked so long in the He can rather than the He will that I have gotten used to the place of incompleteness but He is calling us out of that. He is calling us to swell up in His presence, stand out and be the difference. Quit going along with the "invisible clothes" and call it as it is. We should walk by faith not by sight! We must begin to walk in the reality and not the illusion knowing beyond a shadow of doubt that God is the God of all power and it is His will that you and I be healed! How? Walking in complete confidence of faith that this is the illusion and the reality is His. Miracles still happen...faith is the protuberant factor. There's so much more to say on this but it's a sermon...embrace...study...walk...complete confidence!

I waited and waited and waited for God.
At last he looked; finally he listened.
He lifted me out of the ditch,
pulled me from deep mud.
He stood me up on a solid rock
to make sure I wouldn't slip.
He taught me how to sing the latest God-song,
a praise-song to our God.
More and more people are seeing this:
they enter the mystery,
abandoning themselves to God.

Psalms 40: 1-3

THE ROCK OF WAIT!

One of the hardest things to do as a parent is to not give in to the cries of your kids when you know you are teaching them a lesson, developing their resilience or making them stand up and choose correctly...this requires discipline on your part and teaches discipline to them. It's a necessary growth process. It starts from the moment when they are born as they cry out from anything that is uncomfortable because they haven't developed patience or the ability to manage their own expectations. I remember those cries and how it was so hard to discipline myself and them but the rewards were huge for both of us. This is what David is sharing in this Psalm. He waited and waited while crying out for God to intervene but God had a purpose and when His time was perfect, He looked & He listened. Sometimes we are that hungry baby demanding attention and food at the moment and God hears us but He knows that the time isn't yet. He knows that the indulgence isn't what is best for us because He has a perfect plan. Last year I spent a lot of time in and out of the hospital and after my back surgery when I was in so much pain, I would push that call button wanting those pain meds but the nurses knew that I needed to wean back so as much as it frustrated me, they took their own sweet time getting to me. At the time, in the midst, it made me so irritated and frustrated and whiny and yes, mouthy. I'm sorry to say that, but my body made demands and I wanted it met. They graciously did their job, some even going to the extra mile and getting me heat pads for comfort to stave off the pain until it was time to have more pain relief. I'm sharing that because we are often seeing things through our own lenses of demand and comfort...the human sin nature is all about itself from birth...but God sees more. You may feel like David did, that you are mired or caught in quicksand screaming to God for help and He's ignoring you but that's not it at all. He sees the better plan for you and as a good parent and a faithful God, He is wisely choosing this time and situation to develop you, wean you, strengthen you. He is there. He will not let you drown. He will not let you fall. He may make you go through hard places but He is working within you. This is the gateway to entering the mystery.

The mystery of all that is His. We cannot see "all" with our limited vision because we haven't developed that sense through patience and endurance. You may be caught in a waiting place and you may be screaming out in lusty cries for God to come save you from this situation but rejoice because He is working a work in you. What's the key to entering the mystery? When you can be at peace in the waiting. When you can know with supreme confidence that God has you no matter the situation, you can enter the mystery and see what He has in store. I promise you it is worth the waiting. Take this moment and begin to sing and rejoice in your battle instead of raging and crying. Take the moment to whisper "I trust you Jesus no matter what...even if..." and the door to His mystery will open and you will see past the dark glass to Him face to face. Abandon your will to His. I never let my babies go hungry. I fed them at the right time. They learned that and the fussiness ceased. They became peaceful, trusting me to provide for them. If a baby boy can learn to trust his flawed mother, how can I not learn to trust the Master Creator of this Universe. He can turn the tides that calm this angry sea but He alone decides who enters this mystery...be at calm peace for the Master is at the helm.

"I don't think the way you think.
The way you work isn't the way I work."
God's Decree. "For as the sky soars high
above earth, so the way I work surpasses the
way you work, and the way I think is beyond
the way you think. Just as rain and snow
descend from the skies
and don't go back until they've watered the
earth, Doing their work of making things
grow and blossom,
producing seed for farmers and food for the
hungry, So will the words that come out of my
mouth not come back empty-handed.
They'll do the work I sent them to do,
they'll complete the assignment I gave them.

Isaiah 55: 8-11

THE TREE!

It fascinates me that God in all His ways is recognized by the things in nature for who He is and yet we who are His creation have such a time grasping His ways. The way the pine trees put crosses towards Heaven around the time of Easter seems coincidental to some and yet...the fact that the lumina which is a protein in our bodies which holds our cellular networks together is in the shape of a cross...another coincidence? The dogwood in its growth, many flowers and trees, plants & birds...each recognizing the power of the cross in ways...all coincidences?

God works in ways above our thought processes. Not too long ago I was at a presentation of a study of God in the brain and the scientific community was fascinated because when belief systems were challenged the brain lit up in certain places but when God's name alone was said, the entire brain went silent then lit all at once. God's words alone spoke all of creation into being from "Let there be Light" to "It is finished." His words do not return void or empty. If you are struggling today, cast His words over your life. Speak them in faith believing, for His promises will cover your life and take root. The timing may not be yours, the exact way it happens may not be your way for He does things a little differently. Joseph didn't understand His ways while in prison but God made Him the ruler he had seen in his dreams. Moses went through many years of wandering and battles before he fulfilled the promise of his birth that God had spoken to his mother. Esther didn't understand why she was kidnapped from her family and doubted His ways in her fears but ultimately God used her to save His people.

Your circumstances may seem impossible but He is the God of unseen opportunities hidden in impossible circumstances. Monday night is supposed to bring storms across our nation that we can see and feel but there are many storms beneath the surface that are working His handiwork. His word will not be voided or canceled by a culture or kingdom. His words are eternal. His promises are strong and true. We understand rain, snow, hail & wind are out of our control but within His and He uses these to work His purposes. The storms that come Monday will work a much bigger purpose as they water the crops and birds and flowers giving life before it is seen. His ways...they have unseen purpose. Trust Him. He is doing a good work in you and He is able to complete it. Speak His word, sing His words, they have power and will quell the very storms of life. There is power in His name!